# Solomon's Secret

# Solomon's Secret

## Enjoying Life, God's Good Gift

## RAY C. STEDMAN

MULTNOMAH · PRESS

Portland, Oregon 97266

Cover design by Phil Malyon and Judy Quinn
Photograph by Wayne Aldridge

SOLOMON'S SECRET
© 1985 by Ray C. Stedman
Published by Multnomah Press
Portland, Oregon 97266

Published in cooperation with Discovery Foundation, Palo Alto, California

Edited by Steve Halliday

Printed in the United States of America

Library of Congress Cataloging in Publication Data

Stedman, Ray C.
    Solomon's secret.

    1. Bible. O.T. Ecclesiastes—Commentaries.
I. Title.
BS475.3.S73        1985          223'.807          85-8967
ISBN 0-88070-076-9 (pbk.)

85  86  87  88  89  90  –  10  9  8  7  6  5  4  3  2  1

# Contents

_____

_____

# 1
# THE SEARCH FOR MEANING

Ecclesiastes—mystery book of the Old Testament! Does it teach us to "eat, drink, and be merry," for life will soon be over? Some think it does. Does it deny life after death? Some have read it that way. Why is it the most often-quoted Bible book by atheists and religious skeptics? Certain statements in the book seem to appeal strongly to such scoffers. What shall we make of such a strange book?

We must see one thing right from the beginning: this book is an examination of secular wisdom and knowledge. The book clearly states at the outset that it limits itself primarily to things which are apparent to the natural mind. One of its key phrases is the continual repetition, *under the sun*. "What does a man gain by all the toil at which he toils *under the sun?*" verse 3 asks. We find the phrase used again in verse 9. That is the limitation put upon this book by the author himself.

Ecclesiastes, then, is a summation of what man is able to discern under the sun—that is, in the visible world. The book does consider revelation that comes from beyond man's powers of observation and reason, but only as a contrast to what the natural mind observes. It is an inspired—and accurate—book. It guarantees that what it reports is what people actually believe, even as it makes a searching examination of those beliefs. The book is not merely a collection of ancient philosophies, for what it talks about is very much relevant and up-to-date. Here is what you will hear in soap operas, in political speeches, and in radical or conservative movements of our day. Here is what you will hear both in the halls of academia, and on the streets of any city.

The first three verses introduce the theme of the book:

> *The words of the Preacher, the son of David, king in Jerusalem. Vanity of vanities, says the Preacher, vanity of vanities! All is vanity. What does man gain by all the toil at which he toils under the sun?*

First we learn that the writer is "the Preacher, the son of David, king in Jerusalem." We immediately recognize that this could refer to no one but King Solomon. While "the son of David" could indicate any descendant of David who sat on the throne after him, this particularly describes Solomon, as several things in the book will confirm.

Many of today's critical commentators question Solomonic authorship; very few, in fact, accept it.

They date the book after the Babylonian exile, some 500 years after Solomon died. They do this almost habitually. But their views, based, as they think, upon an examination of the culture of the day, have been proved wrong again and again. Let us, however, begin by accepting that it is indeed Solomon who gives to us in this book the wisdom that God taught him throughout his life.

The translators, unfortunately, refer to Solomon as "the Preacher." I am sorry they used that term. I know the book sounds a bit preachy, especially at the beginning. On reading that second verse it would be easy to affect a "stained-glass" voice, and moan "Vanity of vanities: all is vanity." Modern audiences would immediately tune out.

The word for Preacher is the Hebrew word *Qoheleth*, which means, "one who gathers, assembles, or collects." This is an apt title for the author of this book, who has examined and then collected the philosophies by which men live. The English title "Ecclesiastes" comes from the Greek *ecclesia* or assembly. But perhaps a more helpful English translation would be "the Searcher." Here is a searching mind which has looked over all of life and observed what is behind the actions of people. That is the word which we will use wherever the word, the Preacher, occurs. It is not really a preacher or proclaimer, but a searcher and assembler, that is in view.

You do not have to read the last chapter to find the results of his search, because he puts it right here in verse two: "Vanity of vanities." *Vanity*—that is what he found. Vanity here does not mean pride of face. Many women—and sometimes men— spend a lot of time in front of mirrors. Not only do they finish what they need to do to make themselves presentable, but they take time to admire it. We call that

self-admiration, vanity, pride of face; but that is not
what the Searcher is describing. The original word
here means "emptiness, futility, meaninglessness."
That is what he found. He puts his view of what he
discovered in those terms: Emptiness, a feeling of
futility. That is what life brings.

Nothing in and of itself, the Searcher claims, will
satisfy. No thing, no pleasure, no relationship . . .
none of these have enduring value in life. Perhaps we
could sub-title this study, "The Things That Won't
Work." Everybody is trying to make them work,
everyone has seized on one or another of these philosophies and has tried to make it satisfy him. But according to this Searcher, who has gone through it all,
nothing will work.

When he says, "Vanity of vanities, emptiness of
emptiness," that is the Hebrew way of declaring the
superlative. There is nothing more empty, more
futile, this man concludes, than life.

In verse 3 he asks the question which he constantly
asked throughout his search: "What does man gain
by all the toil at which he toils under the sun?" How
does it profit him? Gain is an interesting Hebrew
word, meaning "that which is left over." After we
have sucked dry all the immediate delight, joy or
pleasure of something, what is left over, what endures, what will remain to continually feed the
hunger of our lives for satisfaction? That is the right
question to ask. It is a question we all are asking. Is
there anything that will minister continually to my
need—that *summum bonum*, that highest good which,
if I find it, I do not need to look any further? Is there
a key to continual pleasure, to delight and joy in life?

The Searcher raises this pertinent question right at
the beginning. It defines the search on which this
book will take us. Verses 4 through 7 describe the

sense of futility which nature gives us as we live, and verses 8 through 11 speak of the frustrations that every individual feels in facing life.

Verses 4-7:

> *A generation goes, and a generation comes, but the earth remains for ever. The sun rises and the sun goes down, and hastens to the place where it rises. The wind blows to the south, and goes round to the north; round and round goes the wind, and on its circuits the wind returns. All streams run to the sea, but the sea is not full; to the place where the streams flow, there they flow again.*

Here are the endless cycles of life. The Searcher states his theme in verse 4: Humanity is transient, but nature is permanent. A generation goes and a generation comes—human beings come into life, live their term and go on—but the earth remains forever.

He gives three examples of this natural phenomenon, the first of which is the circle of the sun. The sun rises in the east, apparently runs across the heavens, and sets in the west; then it scurries around the dark side of the earth while we are sleeping, and there it is in the east again in the morning. That has been going on as long as time has been measured. It is endless. It repeats itself again and again.

Then he speaks of the circuit of the winds from south to north. This is unusual, because we have no evidence that men in Solomon's day understood that the wind, the great jet-streams of earth, run in circles. We see evidence of these great jet-streams every day in the satellite pictures on any TV weather report. Solomon knew it, though the scientific world of that day did not seem to understand it.

His third proof is the evaporative cycle. Thirteen

elders and pastors from our church once spent a few days on a backpack trip to the Sierras. There the mountain peaks milked moisture from the clouds which passed over the dry California coastal plain. Torrents of rain, hail, and even snow fell upon our staff, forcing them to huddle in their little plastic tents. Their question was, "where does all the water which endlessly drops out of the sky come from?" The answer, of course, is that it comes from the ocean. To the west of California an invisible evaporative process is at work so that the water that runs into the sea never raises the level of the sea. That water is invisibly lifted back up into the clouds. The clouds then move east on the circuit of the winds and drop their moisture again. It goes on forever.

The writer suggests here that there is something wrong in all this. It is backwards, somehow. Man ought to be permanent and nature ought to be transient, he suggests. And there is something within each of us that says the same thing. We feel violated when we learn great lessons from life, but just as we have begun to handle life properly it is over, and the next generation has to start from scratch again.

Scripture confirms this racial uneasiness. The Bible tells us that man was created to be the crown of creation. He is the one who is to be in dominion over all things. Men and women ought to last forever and nature ought to be changing—but it is the other way around. We protest this in our spirits. We have all felt it. We resent, inwardly at least, the injustice of losing the wisdom of a Churchill, the beauty of a Princess Grace, or the charm of a John Kennedy. Something is wrong that such value is suddenly taken away from us, while the meaningless cycle of nature goes on and on. Why should this be? It is the question the Searcher continually faced.

Furthermore, the Searcher says, everyone's actual experience confirms this sense of futility.

> *All things are full of weariness ("full of weariness"*
> *is a Hebrew word which ought to be translated*
> *"restless"); a man cannot utter it (describe it); the*
> *eye is not satisfied with seeing, nor the ear filled*
> *with hearing. What has been is what will be, and*
> *what has been done is what will be done; and there*
> *is nothing new under the sun. Is there a thing of*
> *which it is said, "See, this is new"? It has been*
> *already, in the ages before us. There is no remem-*
> *brance of former things, nor will there be any re-*
> *membrance of later things yet to happen among*
> *those who come after (1:8-11).*

His thesis is, "All things are restless." He has observed an inherent restlessness in everything. It is so widespread that nobody can describe it. It permeates all of life, and is found so universally that we are scarcely able to recognize it as an intruder, as an alien to normal human experience.

He has two proofs of this. First, human desire is never satisfied: "The eye is not satisfied with seeing." My wife's mother is 95 years old. She is just a shell of a person now, but her mind is still sharp and clear. The other day we had her in our home and somebody mentioned a far-off place. Immediately she said, "Oh, I wish I could see that." Despite her years, the eye is not tired of seeing; it longs yet to see other places, other realms, other customs. The eye is never satisfied.

Nor is the ear ever satisfied with hearing. We are always alert to some new idea or event. News programs are always popular. Television, radio, and newspapers all cater to this hunger of the ear to hear something new. Juicy gossip about a Hollywood star will sell thousands of magazines and newspapers. That is why we tune in to soap operas. We never tire of hearing something new. Some new way of making a profit always makes its appeal. The Searcher's argument is that the ear never tires because human desire is never satisfied—it is a consequence of the restlessness that is built into life.

But, second, he says, even though we long to see or hear something new, nothing new ever really shows up. Life is a rehash of what has been before; it is the old played over and over again. That is his argument. This too is a result of the restlessness built into life. Although something looks new, actually "there is nothing new under the sun."

Someone immediately objects and says, "Wait a minute! They didn't have radio, television, space travel or any such thing until just a few decades ago. Why even you, Ray Stedman, ought to be able to remember back to the days before they had any of those things!"

When a friend and I were in Hong Kong recently, resting a couple of days after an exhausting travel and speaking schedule, we stayed at the wonderful old British Peninsula Hotel on the Kowloon side of Hong Kong. Right across the street from us was a newly built planetarium, and we went there to see "The Search For Other Civilizations." I'm always excited to sit in those domed rooms. The lights go down, the stars begin to appear above like the stars on a summer's night, and you suddenly feel a sense of eternity, you sense the greatness and magnificence of the universe.

The show began by showing the great statues on Easter Island, in the Pacific Ocean, raising the question, where did these great statues come from? These monoliths are huge, 20 feet or more in height, made of great stones that weigh hundreds of tons. Who erected them? Where did they come from and how did they get there? Then the show took us into areas of South America where huge geometric patterns have been worked out over acres of ground. These designs have obviously been made by man, or some intelligent creature, yet they cannot even be seen unless they are viewed from the sky. This raises the question, Why would any people create figures on the ground so huge that they cannot be seen except from the air? Many have surmised that past civilizations did have ways of rising above the earth. Others suggest that visitors from space used these patterns. Similar mysteries, such as Stonehenge in England, are propounded and compounded as one explores the earth. That planetarium show was a confirmation of what the Searcher of Ecclesiastes declares, "What has been is what will be, and what has been done is what will be done." Other ages will repeat it. "There is nothing new under the sun."

Then why do things appear new? His answer is in verse 11: Man's memory is faulty; we have forgotten things that once were. The planetarium show confirmed that. One excerpt showed the modern Mayan Indians of Central America, the actual blood descendants of a race of intellectual giants who once lived in the area. The ancient Mayans erected temples filled with mysteries that the present generation of Mayans has long forgotten. They cannot explain them: they do not understand them. They have lost the knowledge of the past.

This is what this writer declares. Our memories are so short that we lose what we know—and, he suggests, it may happen again. All these technological marvels that we are so proud of may one day disappear in a great nuclear holocaust. Viewing the remains of our television sets, future generations may well ask, "What is this jungle of wires for? What did they do with this thing?" That is the situation. "There is nothing new under the sun."

So the question is raised: Is this all life is about? Is it merely an empty pursuit after things which never satisfy? Can no breakthrough be made whereby something can be found that will reliably meet the hunger of man's heart, and give an unending sense of delight, satisfaction and joy? That is the search we are on.

Before the Searcher takes us into the details of this search—which begins in chapter 2—he assures us of his qualifications, in verses 12 through 18. These fall into two divisions: his position, and his diligence.

Verses 12-15:

> *I the Searcher have been king over Israel in Jeru-salem. And I applied my mind to seek and to search out by wisdom all that is done under heaven; it is an unhappy business that God has given to the sons of men to be busy with. I have seen everything that is done under the sun; and behold, all is emptiness and a striving after wind. What is crooked cannot be made straight, and what is lacking cannot be numbered.*

This man's position gave him unusual opportunity. He was a king, the highest authority in the land. No one would challenge what he did. And he was a king in a time of peace. For 40 years during the reign of Solomon no armies battered at the walls of Jerusalem, as they had been doing all through its history and are still threatening to do today. His father had amassed great wealth of which Solomon was the heir, and he himself had increased this wealth. For 40 years of the nation's life there was no demand for great military spending. It was a time of peace and great wealth. Furthermore, during this time the Gentile nations were sending delegates to Jerusalem. The Queen of Sheba came all the way from the ends of the earth, she said, to see and hear the wisdom of this man. Solomon had great opportunity to observe life thoroughly.

Furthermore, he was able to investigate widely. "I applied my mind to seek and to search out by wisdom all that is done under heaven," he says. He could get into everything. But with all candor, he has to state, "It is an unhappy business that God has given to the sons of men to be busy with." That translation misses something of what he meant. In the Hebrew it is not "the sons of men," rather, it is "the sons of man." The word is Adam, "the sons of Adam." So the reference is not to the conglomerate of humanity, it is to the nature of man.

I think he is making reference here to the fall of man. He is recognizing the fact that it is difficult for men to discover answers because there is something wrong inside of man. It is a tricky business for a man, who senses an overwhelming curiosity to discover the secrets of life around him, yet he finds himself baffled all the time by an inadequate understanding. Man cannot put it all together.

Furthermore, the Searcher was able to investigate even the opposites of things. "I have seen everything," he says. Yet there were certain limitations inherent in that. That is what he states in a proverb, "What is crooked cannot be made straight, and what is lacking cannot be numbered." It is difficult for man to discover the answers to life, because when he sees something wrong there is yet somehow an inbuilt difficulty that prevents him from correcting it. Have you ever felt, as I have, that when things go wrong in your family, although you long to put them right somehow you cannot get hold of it, you cannot make it right? "That which is crooked cannot be made straight." One of the great frustrations of life is that no matter how hard you try, there are some things you cannot set straight. Also, no matter how much you may discover, there is information you long to have that you cannot obtain. "That which is lacking cannot be numbered." That was this man's problem, and it is ours as well.

Then in verses 16-18 he speaks of his diligence:

> *I said to myself, "I acquired great wisdom, surpassing all who were over Jerusalem before me; and my mind has had great experience of wisdom and knowledge." And I applied my mind to know wisdom and to know madness and folly. I perceived that this also is but a striving after wind. For in much wisdom is much vexation, and he who increases knowledge increases sorrow.*

For students in school, that last statement is a great verse to memorize! "He who increases knowledge increases sorrow." That is true—sad, but true. It is no argument for not increasing knowledge, though, because the alternative is even worse; ignorance is foolishness.

Isn't it remarkable that the Man who for all ages has been the personification of wisdom is also the one who is called "a man of sorrows, and acquainted with grief"? Yet this Searcher kept on, despite the increasing frustration that the more he knew the more he knew he did not know. At the close of his life, Isaac Newton said, "I have but been paddling in the shallows of a great ocean of knowledge." He too felt the frustration of not being able to encompass more.

This last verse gives us a clue to the time when this book was written. It must have been in the latter

years of the reign of Solomon, after he had enjoyed
ample opportunity to investigate all the areas of life
(and had done so). Following that period— which the
book of 1 Kings describes—he fell into spiritual de-
cline, led away by the idolatry of the wives he had
married from foreign nations. This enlightened son
of David, with all his knowledge of the law of Moses
and all the insight of the Word of God, actually ended
up bowing down to lifeless idols in the heathen temples which he built for his wives in Jerusalem! But
there was, apparently, a time of recovery.

One of the Targums of the Jews has an interesting
word here:

> *When King Solomon was sitting upon the throne of
> his kingdom, his heart became greatly elated with
> riches, and he transgressed the commandment of the
> Word of God: and he gathered many houses, and
> chariots, and riders, and he amassed much gold
> and silver, and he married wives from foreign na-
> tions. Whereupon the anger of the Lord was kin-
> dled against him, and he sent to him Ashmodai,
> the king of the demons, and he drove him from the
> throne of his kingdom, and took away the ring
> from his hand, in order that he should roam and
> wander about in the world, to reprove it: and he
> went about the provincial towns and cities in the
> land of Israel, weeping and lamenting, and say-
> ing, "I am Qoheleth, whose name was formerly
> called Solomon, who was king over Israel in Jeru-
> salem."*

There is no reference to this period in Scripture, so
this account may not be trustworthy. But it may be
true! There is suggestion in Scripture that there came
a time when king Solomon saw the folly of what he
was doing, and repented. This book is his considered

proclamation from a chastened mind of what he had learned from life. This is not an angry young man speaking. These are the words of a man who has been through it all and is telling us what he found in his search.

Did he find an answer? Did he find that key to life that makes everything yield up its treasure of joy? Yes, he did, and he tells us the answer in this book. But his answer is not what he began with here. What he found "under the sun" was emptiness—but he went on to find something more than that. That is what this book declares.

# 2
# LIFE IN THE
# FAST LANE

Whether we know it or not, all of us are engaged in a quest for something which will meet the need of our heart. We all are looking for the secret to finding delight anytime, anywhere, and under any circumstances. What we are looking for, in other words, is the secret of contentment. That is the great blessing of life.

That too is what King Solomon was looking for, and in Ecclesiastes he describes his search. We learned from him that there is nothing in and of itself that can make us content. No thing, no possession, no relationship will continually yield up the fruit of contentment and delight.

In chapter 2 we are introduced to the details of this search. Here we have an examination of the various ways by which men through the ages have sought to find contentment and delight in life. The first way, and the one most popular today, is what philosophers call hedonism, the pursuit of pleasure. We all instinctively feel that if we can just have fun we will find happiness. That is what the Searcher examines first.

He starts with what we could well call fun and games.

> *I said to myself, "Come now, I will make a test of pleasure; enjoy yourself." But behold, this also was vanity. I said of laughter, "It is mad," and of pleasure, "What use is it?" I searched with my mind how to cheer my body with wine—my mind still guiding me with wisdom—and how to lay hold on folly, till I might see what was good for the sons of men to do under heaven during the few days of their life (2:1-3).*

Have you ever asked yourself, "What can I do that will make me happy all my life?" That was Solomon's question.

What a time they must have had! Solomon, with all his riches, gave himself completely over to the pursuit of pleasure. He must have spent weeks and months, even years, in this experience.

The first thing he said to himself was, "Enjoy yourself," so he went in for mirth, laughter and pleasure. Let your mind fill in the gaps. Imagine how the palace must have rocked with laughter. Every night there were stand-up comics, and lavish feasts, with wine flowing like water. You may be interested to know what just one day's menu included during this time. First Kings tells us what King Solomon required to feed his retinue in the royal palace for one day.

> *Solomon's provision for one day was thirty cors*
> *of fine flour (a cor is about ten bushels), and sixty*
> *cors of meal (grain of various sorts), ten fat oxen,*
> *and twenty pasture-fed cattle (prime Grade A*
> *meat), a hundred sheep, besides harts, gazelles,*
> *roebucks, and fatted fowl (chickens, ducks, and*
> *all kinds of birds) (1 Kings 4:22-23).*

That was the menu for one day! It has been esti-
mated that it would feed between ten and twenty
thousand people, so there were many others besides
the king involved in this search for pleasure.

Now he tells us what he found. Laughter, he said
to himself, is madness. Perhaps each of us has experienced this to some degree. Have you ever spent an afternoon with a group of your friends, giving yourself
to laughing, having fun, and telling stories about all
kinds of experiences? Most of the stories were based
on exaggeration; they were all embellished a little
and did not have much basis in reality. It is the same
with laughter.

Laughter deals with the peripheries of life. There
is no solid content to it. "The laughter of fools is like
the crackling of thorns under the pot . . . "
(Ecclesiastes 7:6) It is only a crackling noise, that is
all. It leaves one with a sense of unfulfillment. I have
had afternoons and evenings like that which at the
time were delightful. We laughed many times as we
rehashed experiences, and told jokes. But when all
was said and done, we went to bed feeling rather
empty and unfulfilled. That was Solomon's experience. He is not saying that laughter is wrong—and
the Bible does not say that either. It says that laughter is empty; it does not fulfill or satisfy. There is
nothing "left over," no residue that endures.

And what does Solomon say about pleasure?
"What use is it?" What does it contribute to life?

"Nothing" is his answer. Pleasure consumes resources, it does not build them up. Most of us cannot afford a night out more than once or twice a year because it costs so much. Going out uses up resources that hard work has put together. Pleasure, Solomon concludes, adds nothing.

Wine, he adds, is of no help either. It only appears to be so. Every social gathering today almost invariably includes the dispensing of liquor first. The first thing the stewardess says after your plane is airborne is, "Would you like a cocktail?"

There is a widespread conviction in the world that you cannot get strangers to talk to each other until you loosen them up with liquor. And it seems to work. After wine or cocktails are served, people begin to chat a bit and the tenseness and quietness is lessened. But not much of any significance is ever said, either on planes or in social gatherings. There is little communication—usually it is surface conversation. Wine, Solomon says, does not really help. "I looked into it," he says, "and I found that it too was vanity; it left people with a feeling of futility and emptiness."

So he moves to another form of pleasure.

> *I made great works; I built houses and planted vineyards for myself; I made myself gardens and parks, and planted in them all kinds of fruit trees. I made myself pools from which to water the forest of growing trees (2:4-6).*

Here is another form of pleasure—projects, parks, and pools. Many today attempt to find satisfaction in this way. There is pleasure in designing and building a house. In San Jose, California, visitors can tour the Winchester Mystery House, built by a woman who could not stop building. The house is a maze of rooms, doors that open on to blank walls, staircases that go nowhere . . . anything, just to keep on building.

Some wealthy people gain a reputation as philanthropists because they endow beautiful public buildings, always managing to get their names engraved on a brass plaque somewhere in the building. All they are really doing is indulging themselves! It was said of the Emperor Nero that he found Rome a city of bricks and left it a city of marble. But history tells us that his beautification project was not for the benefit of Rome, but for his own gratification and fame.

Solomon too gave himself to this. His own house took fourteen years to build, the temple seven. He built houses for his many wives whom he brought to Jerusalem, spending on them time, money and interest. Southwest of Jerusalem, in a place seldom visited by tourists, there exist today vast depressions in the earth which are still called the Pools of Solomon, which he used to water the forest of trees which he planted in an effort to find satisfaction for his own heart.

Solomon continues to summarize the things which today we could only call "the good life."

> *I bought male and female slaves, and had slaves who were born in my house; I had also great possessions of herds and flocks, more than any who had been before me in Jerusalem. I also gathered for myself silver and gold and the treasure of kings and provinces; I got singers, both men and women, and many concubines, man's delight (2:7-8).*

How modern that sounds! He had servants to wait on every whim. The rich always want somebody else to do all the hard work for them. In this case they were slaves who could not even go on strike if they did not like their circumstances. Solomon had ranches to provide diversion and to make a profit through herds and flocks. Many wealthy people today invest their money in cattle and horse ranches. Bank accounts also give a sense of security. Solomon says he gathered "silver and gold and the treasure of kings and provinces," and brought it all to Jerusalem. He had all the money he needed for his many projects.

Then he had musicians brought in, men and women singers and bands. There were sounds that rivaled the best that we have today. Doubtless the "Jerusalem Pop Orchestra" played concerts under the stars. This is all very up-to-date. We think we have invented this style of living, but here it is in the ancient book of Solomon.

Finally, they had Playmates, girls with bunny tails running around the palace. "Concubines," Solomon calls them, "man's delight!" All the joys of untrammeled sexuality were available at all times. The Playboy mentality is not a twentieth century invention—King Solomon tried all of this.

What did he find? Here are his honest conclusions:

> *So I became great and surpassed all who were before me in Jerusalem; also my wisdom remained with me. And whatever my eyes desired I did not keep from them; I kept my heart from no pleasure, for my heart found pleasure in all my toil, and this was my reward for all my toil. Then I considered all that my hands had done and the toil I had spent in doing it, and behold, all was emptiness and a striving after wind, and there was nothing to be gained under the sun (2:9-11).*

That is very honest reporting. Solomon says he achieved some positive things. First, he gained a degree of notoriety. He became great, surpassing all who went before him in Jerusalem. Many think that fame will satisfy the emptiness of the heart, and Solomon found fame. He adds, though, that he kept his objectivity. "My wisdom remained with me," he says. In other words, "I was able to assess the value of things as I went along. I did not lose myself in this wild search for pleasure. I was able to look at myself and evaluate as I went along. But I tried everything. I did not miss or set aside anything."

He belonged to the jet-set of that day. "I enjoyed it for awhile," he says. "I found pleasure in all my toil," but that was all the reward he got for his labor—momentary enjoyment. Each time he repeated it he enjoyed it a little less. "My conclusion," Solomon suggests, "is that it was not worth it." Like a candle, it all burned away, leaving him jaded and disappointed. Nothing could excite him after that. He concludes that it was "all emptiness, and a striving after wind." He was burned out!

Verses 12 through 23 form a lengthy passage in which the Searcher compares two possible ways of pursuing pleasure. Someone might well come along at this point and say to Solomon, "The reason you ended up so burned out is that you went at this the wrong way. You planned your pleasures, you deliberately gave yourself to careful scheduling of what you wanted to try next. But that is not the way to do it. To really enjoy pleasure, to really live it up, you've got to abandon yourself. Go in for wild, impulsive, devil-may-care pleasure. Do what you feel like doing." Surely this was when the modern motto, "If it feels good, do it" was first advanced.

"All right," Solomon says, "I examined that too."

*So I turned to consider wisdom and madness and folly; for what can the man do who comes after the king? Only what he has already done (2:12).*

By that he means that no one can challenge or contest his judgment in this area because no one could exceed his resources; those who follow him can only repeat what he has done. But after trying it all, here are his conclusions. First:

> *Then I saw that wisdom excels folly as light excels darkness (2:13).*

It is much better to go at it with your eyes open, he says. If you are going to pursue pleasure, at least do not throw yourself into it like a wild man. If you do so you will burn yourself out at the very beginning. You will get involved in things that you cannot imagine. It is like the difference between light and darkness. If there is any advantage to walking in light versus stumbling about in darkness, that is the difference between a wise and careful planning of pleasure and a foolish abandonment to it.

And why should that be?

> *The wise man has his eyes in his head, but the fool walks in darkness . . . (2:14a)*

In other words, the wise man man can foresee some of the results of what he is doing, and he may perhaps avoid them so that the full impact of living for pleasure does not devastate him as fast or as completely as it does the fool. Many have discovered this for themselves. The newspapers every day tell of young people who gave themselves to the wild pursuit of pleasure, and who were soon in jail or burned out with drugs. Solomon says it is better to pursue pleasure according to the way of the wise.

But either way, he says, neither one can avoid death. Here is a very insightful statement at the close of verse 14:

> *. . . and yet I perceived that one fate comes to all of them. Then I said to myself, "What befalls the fool will befall me also; why then have I been so very wise?" And I said to myself that this also is vanity. For of the wise man as of the fool there is no enduring remembrance, seeing that in the days to come all will have been long forgotten. How the wise man dies just like the fool! (2:14b-16).*

It does not really make a lot of difference; in the end they both come to the same fate.

I have often quoted the eloquent words of Lord Bertrand Russell. He was widely regarded as a wise man, although a thoroughgoing atheist and a defender of secular humanism. This was his view of death:

> *One by one as they march, our comrades vanish from our sight, seized by the silent orders of omnipotent death. Brief and powerless is man's life. On him and all his race the slow, sure doom falls, pitiless and dark. Blind to good and evil, reckless of destruction, omnipotent matter rolls on its relentless way. For man, condemned today to lose his dearest, tomorrow himself to pass through the gate of darkness, it remains only to cherish, ere yet the blow falls, the lofty thoughts that ennoble his little days.*

Those words express the truth that the Searcher brings out here. Solomon says that no matter how carefully you pursue life and pleasure it will end in the darkness and dust of death. The fool and the wise man are both forgotten. How many of you knew wise men and women in your past whom no one remembers now? These words are terribly true.

Then he comes to his final, remarkable reaction.

> *So I hated life, because what is done under the sun was grievous to me; for all is vanity and a striving after wind. I hated all my toil in which I had toiled under the sun, seeing that I must leave it to the man who will come after me; and who knows whether he will be a wise man or a fool? Yet he will be master of all for which I toiled and used my wisdom under the sun. This also is vanity. So I turned about and gave my heart up to despair over all the toil of my labors under the sun, because sometimes a man who has toiled with wisdom and knowledge and skill must leave all to be enjoyed by a man who did not toil for it. This also is vanity and a great evil (2:17-21).*

Notice the increasing depression here. First, there is a sense of being grieved, of being hurt by life. "I hated life, because what is done under the sun was grievous to me," the Searcher says. He became increasingly disgruntled when he saw a diminishing return in pleasure for all the effort he made to enjoy life. Have you ever seen people determined to have fun even if it kills them? They try their best to extract from the moment all the joy they can, but they get very little for their efforts. This, Solomon says, was a grief to him.

Second, he was frustrated. "Why do I have to work to put all this together, using all my wisdom and efforts, and eventually have to leave it to some fool coming behind me who will waste it in a few months?" he asks. He is irritated by the unfairness of this.

Finally, he sinks into despair. "I turned about and gave my heart up to despair," he says, because he is helpless to change this law of diminishing returns. This is doubtless an explanation for many of the sudden, unexpected suicides of popular idols, of men and women who apparently had seized the keys to life with riches and fame, and whom the media constantly adored as objects worthy of imitation. But every now and then, finding nothing but frustration and despair as life is used up too quickly and there is no joy left in it, one of these beautiful people takes a gun and blows his brains out.

Think of people like Jack London and Ernest Hemingway. Hemingway's brother committed suicide, as their father had done some years earlier. Think of Freddy Prinz, and of Elvis Presley, who virtually killed himself with drugs. These words which Solomon has faithfully recorded are true; they correspond to life. Emptiness and vexation were Solomon's experience when he tried to live it up without the missing element that his search was focused upon.

So he concludes with this eternal question:

> *What has a man from all the toil and strain with which he toils beneath the sun? For all his days are full of pain, and his work is a vexation; even in the night his mind does not rest. (Insomnia at night, restlessness in his heart, this is what he got under the sun.) This also is emptiness (2:22-23).*

Is there no answer? Is it all hopeless? In the three verses which follow we have the first statement of the true message of this book. Is it but a matter of time before we too are jaded, burned out by excess, life having lost all value, meaning and color? No, says the Searcher. Put a relationship with God into that picture and everything changes. The text says,

> *There is nothing better for a man than that he should eat and drink, and find enjoyment in his toil (2:24).*

Unfortunately here is another instance where we have lost the true meaning of the verse by bad translation. In the next chapter there is a similar passage that properly includes the words, "there is nothing better than," but that is not what it says here. Delete from the text the words, "better than," because they are not in the Hebrew and they do not belong here. What this text actually says is,

> *There is nothing in man that he should eat and drink and find enjoyment in his toil.*

"There is nothing in man," there is no inherent value in him that makes it possible for him to extract true enjoyment from the things he does. That is the first thing Solomon says.

What does, then? He tells us,

> *This also, I saw, is from the hand of God; for apart from him who can eat or who can have enjoyment? (2:24-25)*

Here is the true message of this book. Enjoyment is a gift of God. There is nothing in possessions, in material goods, in money, there is nothing in man himself that can enable him to keep enjoying the things he does. But it is possible to have enjoyment all your life if you take it from the hand of God. It is given to those who please God.

> *For to the man who pleases him God gives wisdom and knowledge and joy . . . (2:26a)*

Wisdom and knowledge have been mentioned before as things you can find "under the sun," but they will not continue. To have added to them the ingredient of pleasure, of continual delight going on and on unceasingly throughout the whole of life, you must take only from the hand of God. To the man who pleases God is given the gift of joy.

It is wonderful to realize that this book—and the whole of the Bible—teaches us that God wants us to have joy. In his letter to Timothy, Paul said, "He gives us richly all things to enjoy" (1 Timothy 6:17). It is God's desire and intent that all the good things of life that are mentioned here should contribute to the enjoyment of man; but only, says this Searcher, if you understand that such enjoyment does not come from things or from people. It is an added gift of God, and only those who please God can find it.

How do you please God? In Hebrews we are told, "Without faith it is impossible to please God" (Hebrews 11:6). It is faith that pleases him, belief that he is there and that all in life comes from his hand. Underscore in your minds the word *all*. Pain, sorrow, bereavement, disappointment, as well as gladness, happiness and joy, all these things are a gift of God. When we see life in those terms then any and every element of life can have its measure of joy—even sorrow, pain, and grief. These things were also given to us to enjoy. That is the message of this book. The writer will develop this further in passages that follow.

You will recognize this is also the message of Romans 8:28: "All things work together for good to those who love God, to those who are called according to his purpose." It is also the message of Proverbs 3:5-6: "Trust in the Lord with all your heart and lean not to your own understanding. In all your ways acknowledge him and he will direct your paths" (NKJV).

The fourth thing which Solomon says here is that all others labor for the benefit of those who please God.

> . . . *but to the sinner he gives the work of gathering and heaping, only to give to one who pleases God* (2:26b).

That explains a remarkable thing that I have observed many times. Privileged as I am to speak in various conference centers around the country, I have often observed that many of these Christian gatherings are held in the expensive homes of millionaires who were not Christians. I am thinking, for instance, of Glen Eyrie, the headquarters of the Navigators, outside Colorado Springs. There in a beautiful natural glade, General William Palmer, founder of Colorado Springs and founder of the Denver and Rio Grande Western Railroad, built an English-style stone castle for his British bride. She never lived in it more than a few weeks, and he himself never enjoyed that property at all. It sat empty for years. Finally it was sold several times and ended up in the hands of the Navigators, who are using it as a Christian conference ground and world headquarters for their training movement.

Twice I have been invited to be conference speaker at a beautiful site on a bluff overlooking the Columbia River in Oregon, an estate called Menucha. This wonderful home, covering almost an acre of ground, was built by a wealthy Jewish businessman who had little interest in spiritual things. He entertained presidents at that home, but now it is in the hands of the Alliance Churches of Oregon.

You can duplicate this kind of story many many times. It is remarkable that God so planned life that these multimillionaires in their pursuit of pleasure spent lavishly on their homes in order that their estates might at last be given into the hands of those who please God! But these lavish spenders will not get anything for all their efforts. This also is vanity and a striving after wind. There is a deep irony about this.

Isn't it strange that the more you run after life, panting after every pleasure, the less you will find, but the more you take life as a gift from God's hand, responding in thankful gratitude for the delight of the moment, the more life seems to come to you? Even the trials, the heartaches and handicaps that others seek to avoid are touched with the blessing of heaven and minister to the heart of the one who has learned to take them from the hand of God.

Fanny Crosby is one of the most popular hymn writers of all time. Blind almost from birth, she lived to be 90 years old. When she was only eight years old she wrote this couplet,

> *Oh, what a happy child I am*
> *Although I cannot see.*
> *I am resolved that in this world*
> *Contented I will be.*

> *How many blessings I enjoy*
> *That other people don't.*
> *To weep and sigh*
> *Because I'm blind,*
> *I cannot and I won't.*

That is the philosophy that pleases God, and that is what the Searcher is talking about here.

All the objections that can be raised against this are going to be examined and tested in the pages that follow. When we finish the book we will find that the Searcher has established without a doubt that joy is a gift of God, and it comes to those who take life daily, whatever it may bring, from the hand of a loving Father.

# 3
# THAT WONDERFUL PLAN FOR YOUR LIFE

What an amazing variety of things are offered to us every day to help us find the secret of successful living!

Magazine articles by the dozens tell us how to cope with various problems. TV commercials—dozens to a program it seems— bombard us, telling us how to be successful in life, or at least how to look successful even if we really aren't. Health clubs offer saunas and whirlpool baths to relax us so we can face life with calm assurance. Scores of drugs are available to turn us on, turn us off, or take us out, whatever.

All this confirms the universal search for the secret of enjoyment. We spend billions of dollars each day on this quest. It is the same quest that the book of Ecclesiastes tells us about. The greatest experiment ever designed to test approaches to success, enjoyment and contentment in life is recorded in this 3,000-year-old book.

We have now come to the third chapter, which describes "opposites" in our experience. "There is a time to weep and a time to laugh," Solomon tells us (verse 4). Throughout this chapter the idea is developed that there is an appropriate time for all of life's experiences.

Have you ever laughed at the wrong time? I have. I was at a funeral once, and the leader asked all present to stand upon their feet. One of my friends whispered to me, "What else could you stand on?" I broke up, and it was very obviously the wrong time to do so. One of our pastors won a kind of immortality for himself at a theological seminary when, on the day of graduation—that most solemn occasion in educational life—he walked down the aisle dressed in his somber graduation robe and holding a coffee cup in his hand. He is remembered in the annals of the seminary as a man who did not practice the appropriate action at the proper time.

But there is an appropriate time for everything, for the unpleasant as well as the pleasant. That is the argument of Ecclesiastes 3. This is not merely a description of what happens in life; it is a description of what God has deliberately planned for us.

Many of us are familiar with the Four Spiritual Laws, the first of which is, "God loves you and has a wonderful plan for your life." When talking to someone about his relationship with God, that is an appropriate place to begin. That is also the plan that is set forth here. All along, Solomon is saying that God longs to bring joy into our lives. Many people think

Ecclesiastes is a book of gloom and pessimism because at the level of the writer's perspective—which, he says, is "under the sun," appraised through the visible things of life—his findings *are* gloomy and pessimistic. But that is not the real message of the book. God intends us to have joy, and his program to bring it about includes all these opposites, both pleasant and painful.

If you look carefully you will see that these eight opening verses gather around three major divisions which correspond to the divisions of our humanity: body, soul, and spirit. The first four pairs deal with the body:

> *For everything there is a season, and a time for every matter under heaven: a time to be born, and a time to die; a time to plant, and a time to pluck up what is planted; a time to kill, and a time to heal; a time to break down, and a time to build up (3:1-3).*

Notice how truly those apply to physical life. None of us asked to be born; it was something done to us, apart from our will. None of us ask to die; it is something done to us by God. So we should view this list of opposites as a list of what God thinks we ought to have. It begins by pairing birth and death as the boundaries of life "under the sun."

The next pair speaks of the food supply. "A time to plant and a time to harvest." Everything must come in its appropriate time. If you get it out of sync you are in trouble. Try to plant a crop in the middle of winter when snow is on the ground and it will not grow. Half of the problem of life is that we are constantly trying to run this schedule ourselves. But God has already planned the schedule. There is an appropriate time for everything.

There is "a time to kill, and a time to heal." That may sound strange to us, but the process of dying goes right along with the process of living. Doctors tell us that every seven years all the cells in our bodies but the brain cells die. But our bodies do not die. What you are now is not what you were seven years ago, yet you are somehow the same. Man's physical body is one of the miracles of the universe. As the psalmist says, "We are fearfully and wonderfully made."

How can we understand that each cell seems to pass on to the cell which replaces it the memory of the past so that the memory goes back beyond the life of the cell itself? There is "a time to kill, and a time to heal." God brings both to pass.

There is "a time to break down, and a time to build up." Youth is the time for building up. Muscles grow, abilities increase, coordination gets better. Then if you hang on long enough and reach that sixty-fifth milestone, there is a time when everything starts to fall apart—"a time to break down." Type gets smaller and smaller, steps get higher and higher, trains go faster and faster, people speak in lower and lower tones—"a time to break down." But that is appropriate. We should not resent it. It is not evil; it is right. God has determined this, and no matter what we may think about it, it is going to continue. That is what this tells us.

Then the Searcher moves into the realm of the soul, with its functions of thinking, feeling and choosing. He moves into the social areas, and all the interrelationships of life that flow from that. "A time to weep, and a time to laugh; a time to mourn, and a time to dance" (3:4). All these things follow closely, and all are appropriate. No one is going to escape the hurts and sorrows of life, because God *chose* them for us. The proof of that is in the coming of God's own Son. He was not handed a beautiful life, everything pleasant and delightful, free from struggle and pain. No. He was "a man of sorrows and acquainted with grief." In a fallen world it is right that there will be times of hurt, of sorrow and weeping.

But there will be other times when it is right to laugh, to be happy and carefree. There is a time of grief and tears—"a time to mourn"—but there is another time to celebrate and to enjoy festive occasions. Jesus celebrated a wedding at Cana of Galilee. He entered into it and even provided part of the feast.

Then there is "a time to cast away stones, and a time to gather stones together" (3:5a). There is a time to break things down, and a time to build them up again. This has to do particularly with our social structures, with our relationships to others. There is a time when we need to embrace others, to show our support for them. But there are other times when we ought to refuse to embrace them, when our support would be misunderstood and would be tantamount to complicity with evil. All those occasions come from the hand of God.

The last six of these opposites relate to the spirit, to the inner decisions, the deep commitments. There is "a time to seek (work, marriage, new friends), and a time to lose" (3:6a). There comes a time when we should curtail certain friendships, or change our jobs, or move away, and lose what we had in the past. It is proper and appropriate that these times should come.

There is "a time to keep and a time to cast away" (3:6b). There are values and standards which must never be surrendered, while there are other times when we need to throw away things—clean out the attic, the garage, throw away the old clothes. This can be true of habits and attitudes.

Resentments need to be thrown away. Grudges and long-standing hurts need to be forgiven and forgotten.

There is "a time to keep silence, and a time to speak" (3:7b). There are times when we know something, a piece of gossip perhaps, and we should not say it. We should keep silent. There are other times when we ought to speak, when something we are keeping secret would deliver someone or bring truth into a situation; there is a time to speak up.

There is "a time to love, and a time to hate" (3:8a). When is it time to hate? Think of young Abraham Lincoln the first time he saw human beings sold on the slave blocks in New Orleans. He felt hatred rising in his heart. He resolved that if he ever got a chance to smash slavery he would do so. Lincoln's hatred of slavery was perfectly appropriate. There is "a time to love," when it is right that we should extend our love to somebody who is hurting, someone who is feeling dejected or rejected, lonely or weak.

There is "a time for war, and a time for peace" (3:8b). We ought to remember this as we consider some of the issues before us. When tyranny rides roughshod over the rights of men there is a time when a nation properly makes war. But there is a time when war is absolutely the wrong thing, when no provocation should be allowed to start one, because war can explode into violence far beyond anything demanded by the situation. How much is permitted in that regard is widely debated today.

I point out that all of this is God's wonderful plan for your life. The problem, of course, is that it is not *our* plan for our life. If we were given the right to choose, we would have no unpleasantness at all in life. But that would ruin us. God knows that people who are protected from everything invariably end up impossible to live with; they are selfish, cruel, vicious, shallow, unprincipled. God sends these things in order that we might learn. There is a time for everything, the Searcher says.

But more than that . . . if God has a time for everything, he also has certain unchanging principles which we must take into account in everything, as this next passage declares.

*What gain has the worker from his toil? (3:9).*

What is "left over" to provide a permanent sense of satisfaction after we extract the momentary pleasure from some pleasurable experience? That is the question which underlies all of the Searcher's examinations. He has already asked it three times in this book. The answer follows:

*I have seen the business that God has given to the sons of men to be busy with (3:10).*

Life itself reveals the secret. The principles behind things can be found by careful, thoughtful examination, something Solomon has been making all along.

Now he gives that answer. He found three things. First,

*He has made everything beautiful in its time (3:11a);*

We have already looked at that. Everything is appropriate and helpful to us, even what appears to be negative. These are not curses and obstacles; they are God's blessings, deliberately provided by him.

Even our enemies are a blessing. I received a letter from a businessman friend of mine in Dallas, a very thoughtful man. He gave me his thinking along this line, saying that there were five types of people whom he had learned from in life: "heroes, models, mentors, peers and friends." He continued:

*I have added another: Enemies. They have a very important place in our lives. Enemies are the opposite bank of our existence. We define our position partly by theirs, as light is the opposite of darkness, of course. They plumb the depth of our Christian maturity, exposing our self centeredness, self-righteousness and arrogance. They attack and expose our motives, for seldom do we form an enemy out of a mere mistake of fact or even opinion. Enemies are personal, not positional. Therefore, as a personal matter we are commanded to love them. This command is like a spiritual thermometer stuck into the depths of our feverish little souls. It is interesting that the Jewish historian and sociologist Hart puts this command as the greatest difference between Christianity and all other world religions.*

"Love your enemies," Jesus said, partly because they are valuable to you. They do something for you that you desperately need. Our problem is that we have such a shallow concept of things. We want everything to be smooth and pleasant. More than that, we want to be in charge, we want to limit the term of hurt or pain. But God will not allow us to take his place and be in charge. There is rhythm to life which even secular writers recognize. The book *Passages* speaks of the various experiences we pass through as we grow and mature.

The second thing the Searcher learned in his search is:

*also he has put eternity into man's mind . . . (or literally, "man's heart") (3:11b).*

There is a quality about humanity that can never be explained by evolution. No animal is restless and dissatisfied when its physical needs have been met.

Observe a well fed dog sleeping before the fire on a cold day. He is with his family, enjoying himself, not worried about anything. Put a man in that position and soon he will feel a sense of restlessness. There is something beyond, something more that he cries out for. This endless search for an answer beyond what we can feel or sense physically or emotionally is what is called here "eternity in man's heart." St. Augustine prayed, "Thou has made us for Thyself, and our hearts are restless until they learn to rest in Thee."

Man is the only worshiping animal. What makes us different cannot be explained by evolution. We are different because we long for the face of God. C.S. Lewis said, "Our Heavenly Father has provided many delightful inns for us along our journey, but he takes great care to see that we do not mistake any of them for home." There is a longing for home, there is a call deep in the human spirit for more than life can provide. This itch which we cannot scratch is also part of God's plan.

The third thing which the Searcher learned is that mystery yet remains:

> *. . . yet so that he cannot find out what God has done from the beginning to the end (3:11c).*

We are growing in our knowledge, but we discover that the more we know, the more we know we do not know. The increase of knowledge only increases the depth of wonder and of delight. In the sovereign wisdom of God we cannot solve all mysteries. As the apostle Paul put it, "we see through a glass darkly"; we are looking forward to the day when we shall see face-to-face.

We cannot know all the answers to the conundrums and enigmas of life. The exhortation of Scripture is always to trust the revelation of the Father's wisdom in areas we cannot understand. Jesus said over and over that the life of faith is like that of a child. A little child in his father's arms is unaware of many things that his father has learned. But, resting in those arms, he is quite content to let the enigmas unfold as he grows, trusting in the wisdom of his father.

That is the life of faith, and that is how we are to live. In verses 12 through 15 we learn the purpose of God in this remarkable plan. Three things are found here. First:

> *I know that there is nothing better for them than to be happy and enjoy themselves as long as they live . . . (3:12).*

Everybody agrees with that. That is what the commercials tell us: "Live life with gusto. You only go around once. Seize it now." All right. The Searcher says so too!

Secondly, he says:

> *also that it is God's gift to man that every one should eat and drink and take pleasure in all his toil (3:13).*

Underline the words, "take pleasure." That is what the Searcher finds that man cannot produce. Things in themselves give a momentary—not lasting—pleasure. True enjoyment is the gift of God; it is what God wants. That is what the Searcher has been arguing all along.

How different is this picture from what most people think life is like under the sovereign Lordship of a Living God! I saw a book on sex the other day entitled *Intended for Pleasure*. That is true, sex is designed for pleasure. But it is not merely sex that is designed for pleasure—all things are designed for human pleasure! But if you think the thing in question is going to produce lasting pleasure, you will miss it. The secret is that it is only a vibrant relationship with God that produces enjoyment.

We are not in the grasp of a Great Cosmic Joykiller, as many people seem to view God. God delights in human enjoyment.

The third thing the Searcher says is that it all must be discovered by realizing that God is in charge and he will not bend his plan for anyone.

> *I know that whatever God does endures for ever; nothing can be added to it, nor anything taken from it; God has made it so . . . (3:14a).*

God has sovereignly and independently, set up the plan of life in a way that cannot be interfered with. He has done so "in order that men should fear before him" (3:14b).

All through the Bible we read that "The fear of the Lord is the beginning of wisdom." Until we recognize and trust the superior wisdom of God we have not begun to fear God. This fear is not abject terror of God, it is respect and honor for him. If you try to live your life without recognizing God, ultimately you will find yourself (as the Searcher found himself) empty, dissatisfied and restless, feeling that life is miserable and meaningless. The secret of life is the presence of God himself.

Most of life's struggle comes when we want to play God ourselves, when we want to be in charge. That is true even of Christians. When God refuses to go along we sulk and pout and get angry with him. We throw away our faith and say, "What's the use? I tried it but it doesn't work!" What foolishness! God will not surrender his prerogatives: "Nothing can be added to it, nor anything taken from it; God has made it so in order that men should fear before him."

Solomon says that God will teach this through much repetition.

> *That which is, already has been; that which is to be, already has been; and God seeks what has been driven away (3:15).*

A better translation of that last phrase is, "God brings back what has already passed away."

The Searcher here refers to the repetition of life's lessons. We do not seem to learn very well. I have learned some lessons in life and said, "Lord, I see what you are after. I've got it now. You don't have to bring this one back again." But down the road I make the same mistake. Some circumstance painfully recalls to mind what I had once seen as a principle in life. I have to humbly come and say, "Lord, I'm a slow learner. Have patience with me." God says, "I understand. I'm prepared to have patience with you and teach you this over and over and over again until you get it right."

Have you found life to be like that? The Searcher tells us that he too had to learn this. That is the Searcher's thesis. God wants us to learn the secret of enjoyment. That enjoyment will not come from many experiences. Those will bring but momentary pleasure—not the secret of contentment, of continual enjoyment.

A plaque on my bedroom wall, which I read every morning, says:

> *No thought is worth thinking*
> *that is not the thought of God.*
>
> *No sight is worth seeing*
> *unless it is seen through his eyes.*

> *No breath is worth breathing*
> *without thanks to the One*
> *Whose very breath it is.*

It is this continual recognition of the hand of God in ordinary events which fills the springs of enjoyment and gives lasting pleasure.

Verse 16 of chapter 3 begins a section which runs through chapter 5, in which a series of objections to Solomon's thesis are examined. One by one Solomon considers the circumstances that seem to challenge his thesis.

Someone may say, "Wait a minute. You say that God has a wonderful plan for my life, that he is a God of justice. But last week I was seeking justice in a courtroom and I found that the cards were stacked against me; all I got was the rawest injustice. How do you square that with this 'wonderful plan for my life?'" The Searcher takes this up first.

> *Moreover I saw under the sun that in the place of justice, even there was wickedness, and in the place of righteousness, even there was wickedness (3:16).*

Courtrooms are designed to correct injustice, but they are often filled with wickedness and injustice. Recently I was a witness in a case in which a man's business was being destroyed by legal maneuverings. Everyone knew this was unjust, but certain legalities prevented anyone from getting hold of the matter to correct it. That kind of injustice can create anger and frustration. People say, "What do you mean, I am to accept that as from the hand of God?"

The Searcher examines this and says there are three things he wants to show us about it. First:

> *I said in my heart, God will judge the righteous
> and the wicked, for he has appointed a time for
> every matter, and for every work (3:17).*

Though there is present injustice, that is not the
end of the story. God may correct it even within time;
but if he does not do so in this life, still he has appointed a time when everything will be brought out.
The Scriptures speak of a time appointed by God
when the hidden motives of the heart will be
examined, when "that which is spoken in secret shall
be shouted from the housetops," and justice will ultimately prevail. That is what this Searcher declares.
Injustice is limited in its scope. It will ultimately be
judged.

Second:

> *I said in my heart with regard to the sons of men
> that God is testing them to show them that they are
> but beasts (3:18).*

He recognizes there is a beastly quality about all of
us which injustice will bring out. What is it about a
man that makes him prey upon even his friends or
neighbors? On the TV program "The People's
Court," one case concerned a young woman who had
gotten angry at her friend and roommate, whom she
had known for years. In her anger she had poured
sugar into the woman's car's gas tank, destroying the
engine. The judge was appalled at the vindictive
spirit of this attractive young woman who had acted
in such a vicious way.

There is a beastliness about us all. Put in a situation where we are suffering injury, we react with vic-
iousness. God often allows injustice to show us that
we all have that quality about us.

We are like animals in other ways, too, the
Searcher says.

> *For the fate of the sons of men and the fate of
> beasts is the same; as one dies, so dies the other.
> They all have the same breath and man has no ad-
> vantage over the beasts; for all is vanity. All go to
> one place (not hell—he is talking about the grave);
> all are from the dust, and all turn to dust again
> (3:19-20).*

Man is frail, his existence temporary. Like the animals, we do not have very long to live on this earth.
Injustice sharpens the realization that we are on an
earth where, like animals, we must put up with unpleasant circumstances. We die like an animal and
our bodies dissolve like a beast's. From the human
standpoint one cannot detect any difference. So the
Searcher says:

> *Who knows whether the spirit of man goes up-
> ward and the spirit of the beast goes down to the
> earth? (3:21).*

That really should not be a question as it is stated
in this text. It should read this way:

> *Who knows that the spirit of man goes upward
> and the spirit of the beast goes down to the earth.*

That is something which only revelation can tell
us. Experience cannot offer any help at all here. From
a human standpoint, a dead man and a dead dog look
as if the same thing happened to both of them. But
from the divine point of view that is not the case.
Though we die like beasts, the spirit of man goes up-
ward while the spirit of the beast goes downward.
Later on the Searcher states very positively that at
death the spirit of man returns to God who gave it,
but the spirit of the beast ends in nothingness. Injustice stems from our beastliness, and God's plan for
life will uncover it through adverse events.

Finally, he concludes in verse 22:

> *So I saw that there is nothing better than that a man should enjoy his work, for that is his lot; who can bring him to see what will be after him?*

He does not answer that question here; he leaves it hanging. But the answer, of course, is that only God can help us to understand what lies beyond this life.

The wonderful thing to extract from this passage is the great truth that God wants us to handle life in such a way that we can rejoice in every circumstance. Recognize that everything comes from a wise Father. Though circumstances bring us pain as well as pleasure, it is his choice for us. Rejoice that in the midst of the pain there is the possibility of pleasure.

# 4
# WHY DOES GOD ALLOW THIS?

In Ecclesiastes 4 and 5, the ancient Searcher of Israel answers a question all of us have asked at one time or another. Whenever a tragedy occurs, or a terrible injustice is revealed, someone is sure to remark, "You say your God is a God of love, but how could a God of love allow such a thing to happen?"

How, after all, could a God of love allow thousands of innocent Indians to die choking from poison gas? How could a God of love sit by and watch as husbands, wives, sons and daughters fry to death in the crash of a faulty commuter airline? Sometimes the question is more personal: "How can you say God loves me when he lets me work my fingers to the bone and allows other people who have inherited wealth spend their days enjoying themselves?"

In chapter 3 the Searcher declared that God has a wonderful plan for each life. There is a time for everything: "a time to be born, and a time to die; a time to weep, and a time to laugh." Solomon thereby declared that God has a perfect plan including everything that we need, the painful as well as the pleasant.

If we accept both as God's choices for us, as coming from his loving heart—not out of anger nor out of desire to punish, but out of love—we will discover three wonderful things. First, we will be enabled to enjoy all of life, even the painful things. Second, we will learn to know God. Jesus said, "This is eternal life, that they may know thee, the only true God, and Jesus Christ whom thou hast sent" (John 17:3). We will satisfy the sense of eternity which God has put in each heart. That will happen when our attitude toward life changes with a new relationship with God. Third, this lesson will be repeated until we learn it, until we get it right.

There follows immediately four frequently voiced objections that appear to contradict the idea that God has a wonderful plan for everyone. We looked at the first in the last chapter—that injustice thrives where justice ought to be found, in the courts and judicial systems of our land. Recently the newspapers told of a man who spent five years in jail for another man's crime. When this was discovered he was freed, but was given nothing for his time in jail. That sort of injustice raises the question, "What do you mean, 'God has a perfect plan for our lives?' How can you square that statement with such an injustice?"

The Searcher gives us two answers. One, we must remember that the final recompense lies ahead; God has appointed a time when he will bring to light all the hidden things and straighten them out. Second, even injustice teaches us something of great value—it reveals the beastliness we share with the animals. Not only do we have a temporary existence like the animals, but we share with the animals a beastly quality which injustice will bring out.

In chapter 4 the Searcher discusses three more objections to the idea that God has a wonderful plan for our lives. First, he ponders oppression in society:

> *Again I saw all the oppressions that are practiced under the sun. And behold, the tears of the oppressed, and they had no one to comfort them! On the side of their oppressors there was power, and there was no one to comfort them. And I thought the dead who are already dead more fortunate than the living who are still alive; but better than both is he who has not yet been, and has not seen the evil deeds that are done under the sun (4:1-3).*

Oppression almost invariably preys on the helpless, the weak and the infirm, those who cannot defend themselves. The Searcher knows this. Notice how he records the anguish, the misery that it causes. He speaks of "the tears of the oppressed," of the weeping, of the sorrow and brokenness which the oppressed feel over something they can do nothing about. Then he twice categorizes the awful sense of helplessness that oppression evokes. There is no one to comfort the oppressed in a world filled with injustice. The hopeless and the helpless ask, "Who can we turn to? Where can we go for deliverance?" They believe that death would be preferable to what they are going through; they even come to the point where they wish they had never been born. Job felt that way. "Let the day perish wherein I was born," he said. "Why did I not die at birth?" (Job 3).

How do you square that with the glib declaration, "God has a wonderful plan for your life"? How can you say that to someone who is being oppressed? The Searcher does not attempt to answer that for the moment. He records it and sympathizes, but for the moment, he leaves it be.

First, he looks at another objection, that envy and ambition really are the driving force behind man's activity, rather than the enjoyment of life.

> *Then I saw that all toil and all skill in work come from a man's envy of his neighbor. This also is vanity and a striving after wind (4:4).*

How accurately this records what actually happens! People really do not want things, they want to be admired for the things they have. What they want is not the new car itself, but to hear their neighbors say, "How lucky you are to have such a beautiful car!" That is what people want—to be the center, the focus of attention.

I clipped from *Newsweek* magazine an article on life in Washington, D.C. This is what the reporter says drives people in the nation's capital:

> *Ambition is the raving and insatiable beast that most often demands to be fed in this town. The setting is less likely to be some posh restaurant or glitzy nightclub than a wholly unremarkable glass office building, or an inner sanctum somewhere in the federal complex. The reward in the transaction is frequently not currency at all, but power, perquisites, and ego massage. For this, the whole agglomeration of psychological payoffs, there are people who will sell out almost anything, including their self-respect, if any, and the well-being of thousands of others.*

That says exactly what Solomon is saying. The drive to be admired is the true objective of many lives. But, he says, this too "is vanity and a striving after wind." It will not give lasting enjoyment.

Sometimes when people become aware of this they flip over to the opposite extreme. They drop out of society, they get out of the rat race, they go on relief and let the government support them. We saw that kind of reaction in California in the 60s. Young people, particularly, were saying, "We don't want to be a part of the rat race any more; we don't want to make money or play games to be admired. We'll drop out instead!" But that is not the answer either, the Searcher says.

> *The fool folds his hands, and eats his own flesh (4:5).*

Many young men and women who were part of the counter culture of a decade ago have found this to be true—that when you sit in idleness you devour yourself, your resources disappear, your self-respect vanishes. They had to learn the painful lesson that the only way to maintain themselves, even physically (let alone psychologically), was to go to work and stop devouring their own flesh.

It would be much better, says the Searcher, to lower your expectations and choose a less ambitious lifestyle.

> *Better is a handful of quietness than two hands full of toil and a striving after wind (4:6).*

Yet so powerful is ambition and the desire to be envied, he says, that men actually keep working and toiling even when they have no one to leave their riches to.

> *Again, I saw vanity under the sun: a person who has no one, either son or brother, yet there is no end to all his toil, and his eyes are never satisfied with riches, so that he never asks, "For whom am I toiling and depriving myself of pleasure?" This also is vanity and an unhappy business (4:7-8).*

How true! Some people keep on toiling although they have no one to work for, and nothing to do with the money they make. They even deny themselves the pleasures of life in order to keep on amassing funds. What a sharp example was given to us in the story of the late billionaire Howard Hughes.

He did not know what to do with his money. His heirs, who have been impossibly difficult to identify for certain, were left to squabble over it. Somehow in all his tragic existence, the man never seemed to ask himself, "Why am I doing this? What is life all about? Why am I amassing these tremendous amounts of money when I don't even spend a dime on myself?" Such is the folly of toiling for riches out of ambition and ego.

In contrast, the Searcher admits that companionship is better than loneliness.

> *Two are better than one, because they have a good reward for their toil. For if they fall, one will lift up his fellow; but woe to him who is alone when he falls and has not another to lift him up. Again, if two lie together, they are warm; but how can one be warm alone? And though a man might prevail against one who is alone, two will withstand him. A threefold cord is not quickly broken (4:9-12).*

Someone may say, "It's true that men work out of a sense of ambition and a drive for admiration from others, but companionship is useful while doing so."

The Searcher agrees, and lists four advantages to this. First, having a partner will increase the reward. Two really can live cheaper than one. Many people get married on that basis. During the Depression there was a popular song that said, "Potatoes are cheaper, tomatoes are cheaper, now's the time to fall in love."

Many young people agreed with that and got married. But the economy has changed. Today "potatoes are dearer, tomatoes are dearer" . . . but still "now is the time to fall in love" because you can combine your resources. Even the IRS recognizes the advantage of this by giving tax breaks to couples.

Second, the Searcher says, a friend will help in times of trouble. If you get into difficulty your friend or roommate will be there to help you.

You have to have grown up in Montana to fully appreciate the third advantage! When the temperature is 40 degrees below zero outside, you understand what the Searcher means when he says, "If two lie together, they are warm; but how can one be warm alone?" Even at the physical level, companionship is an advantage.

Fourth, the presence of another or more than one other in your life makes defeat unlikely: "A man might prevail against one but two will withstand him, and a threefold cord is not quickly broken."

Still, while there are advantages in companionship, the Searcher's argument nevertheless is that it adds up to emptiness; it does not satisfy the sense of eternity that God has put in men's hearts. Many a couple sit in loneliness, staring at a television screen for hours at a time, or seek some other diversion to fill the emptiness and misery of their lives. No . . . companionship, though better than loneliness, is not the answer either.

A final objection is raised in the latter part of chapter 4. This says, in effect, that living a long life does not always guarantee that one will learn the secrets of enjoyment. The Searcher has been saying that God has a perfect plan and he will teach you as you go; if you live long enough and listen carefully you will learn that enjoyment is a gift of God. But now someone argues that he knows people who live a long time who still do not seem to learn this.

> *Better is a poor and wise youth than an old and foolish king, who will no longer take advice, even though he had gone from prison to the throne or in his own kingdom had been born poor (4:13-14).*

Age can make you headstrong and fanatical, convinced that everything you want to do is right. Even living a long time does not teach us all the lessons, although a long life usually does teach much. But all of us know people who ought to know better, people who have forgotten the lessons they learned in their youth. Here was a king who had gone from prison to the throne because he understood life; he had been poor and he was exalted to a position of power, but he forgot all the lessons he had learned. Compared to him, even a callow youth is preferable.

The Searcher's second argument is that even the wise youth will go on to repeat the same error.

> *I saw all the living who move about under the sun, as well as that youth, who was to stand in his place; there was no end of all the people; he was over all of them. Yet those who come later will not rejoice in him. Surely this also is vanity and a striving after wind (4:15-16).*

Here is a young man who went through the same difficulties as the old king had. He won his way to popularity and power, yet he did not learn either. Although he had the example of his predecessor, he ultimately lost the respect of others. So time does not always teach us the right lessons. All of it remains "vanity, emptiness, a striving after wind."

In chapter 5, a marvelous chapter, the Searcher answers these objections. He declares four things. First:

> *Guard your steps when you go to the house of God (5:1a);*

That is, learn to let God be God; this is the first thing he suggests. The lessons of life will fall into place when you learn it. God is in charge of life, so let him be in charge.

The place to learn this is in the house of God. When you go there, guard your steps—enter thoughtfully, meditatively, expect to be taught something. In ancient Israel the house of God was the Temple in Jerusalem. There sacrifices were offered along with explanations of what they meant. There the law was read, and the wisdom of God about life was declared. This marvelous Old Testament was unfolded, with its tremendous insights into the truth about life and humanity. The Temple was the only place in the land where people could learn these things.

In our day the house of God is no longer a holy building. We must be clear about that. We, believing people, are the house of God! What the Searcher is saying is that when we gather as the people of God, be expectant; there is something to be learned, something important. Being with the people of God is important to learning to let God be God.

Second, he says, listen carefully:

> *. . . to draw near to listen is better than to offer the sacrifice of fools: for they do not know that they are doing evil (5:1b).*

A fool is someone who glibly utters naive, ingenuous, and usually false things. What the Searcher clearly has in mind here is that human tendency to complain and murmur about what has been handed us in life. When we grouse about our circumstances we are really complaining against God. We are murmuring against the choice God has made in his wonderful plan for our life.

We will never learn to enjoy anything by complaining. We will not even enjoy our pleasures, let alone our pain. So he says, "listen carefully," for among the people of God the truth of God is being declared; the wisdom of God is being set forth.

Recently in church a man said to me, "I have been going through a painful experience this past week. I learned to see myself and it horrified me. I saw things in myself which I despise in others." That is encouraging, for that man is learning truth about himself.

The Searcher continues:

> *Be not rash with your mouth, nor let your heart be hasty to utter a word before God, for God is in heaven, and you upon earth; therefore let your words be few. For a dream comes with much business, and a fool's voice with many words (5:2-3).*

It is easy to take the phrase, "God is in heaven," to mean that God is far off somewhere, high above the universe and watching the affairs of men while we insignificant pygmies struggle along down here. But that is not what this means. Heaven is not some distant place. In the Bible, heaven means the invisible world of reality, the arena in which things are going on that we cannot see, but yet is really here. God is in that realm, and he sees much more than we do.

As a preacher, when I look out on a congregation I

see bodies. They reveal certain things—some are interested, some are asleep. But if I were to pray for those people, there is no way I could understand the complexity and depth of struggle that many are going through.

But God sees. God not only sees your body, he sees what is inside, even what you cannot see. He sees every one that way. Remember that when you are coming to God. When he speaks through his Word, that Word is much more true than anything you can imagine as an explanation of life, because God sees all of life from beginning to end. He is in heaven and you are upon earth, so for heaven's sake, don't start griping about what God has handed you! That is the Searcher's argument.

The saints have had to learn this lesson from time immemorial. It is reflected in a hymn by William Cowper:

> *God moves in a mysterious way*
> *His wonders to perform:*
> *He plants his footsteps in the sea,*
> *And rides upon the storm.*
> *Deep in unfathomable mines*
> *Of never ending skill,*
> *He treasures up his bright designs,*
> *And works his sovereign will.*
> *You fearful saints, fresh courage take!*
> *The clouds you so much dread,*
> *are big with mercies, and shall break*
> *In blessings on your head.*

"God is in heaven and you upon earth; therefore let your words be few." Then the Searcher adds, "For a dream comes with much business." By "dreams" he means fantasies, and fantasizing produces much activity but accomplishes nothing. So also a fool with

his many words of complaint accomplishes nothing.
Again, he says, "Don't play games with God."

> *When you vow a vow to God, do not delay pay-*
> *ing it: for he has no pleasure in fools. Pay what*
> *you vow (5:4).*

God is a realist. He never plays games with us. He
sees things the way they really are and he tells us the
way they are. God expects us to carry out our word
when we give it. It is dangerous to make superficial
promises about what we will do if he will only do this
or that. He hears our promises, and he takes us at our
word. There is a penalty when we do not keep it. This
warns us to be careful about what we promise God.
Do not make rash vows, for he is not pleased with
fools.

In fact, the Searcher goes on to say:

> *It is better that you should not vow than that*
> *you should vow and not pay. Let not your mouth*
> *lead you into sin, and do not say before the mes-*
> *senger (the priest or pastor, the representative of*
> *God) it was a mistake . . . (5:5-6a).*

Do not say when the shoe begins to pinch, "I
didn't really mean that." How many have said this
about wedding vows! But God takes you at your
word. "It was all a mistake," they say, "I didn't know
what I was doing." But the Searcher warns,

> *. . . why should God be angry at your voice,*
> *and destroy the work of your hands? For when*
> *dreams increase, empty words grow many: but do*
> *you fear God (5:6b-7).*

We are dealing with the Author of life itself. He
holds our lives in the palm of his hand. God is not
cruel and heartless; he *is* loving, but he is real, so do

not play games with him. Be honest with God; that is all the Searcher is saying. Pay attention when you hear the words of God. Listen as he describes life to you. He is telling you these things so that you might find enjoyment in all that you do.

Third, value government, for it too is from God.

> *If you see in a province the poor oppressed and justice and right violently taken away, do not be amazed at the matter (do not be angry and bitter over this); for the high official is watched by a higher, and there are yet higher ones over them. But in all, a king is an advantage to a land with cultivated fields (5:8-9).*

The argument is very simple: do not be astonished and bitter at injustice. God has set up higher officials who may correct oppression when they become aware of it. But even if they do not, there is One yet higher. He is aware, and he knows what he is doing. Recognize that there is good in government. It has been well said, "Even bad government is better than no government at all." We cannot live in anarchy. Even the worst kind of government is better than no government, so value it. Such an attitude will greatly help in dealing with the problems of life.

Finally, the Searcher deals with a fourth circumstance. Most people feel that if they could only get rich, they could handle the pressures better. The Searcher examines that more closely in verses 10 through 17.

> *He who loves money will not be satisfied with money; nor he who loves wealth, with gain: this also is vanity (5:10).*

First, money will not satisfy, for money does not leave you feeling full and enjoying life. There is plenty of testimony to that today from the rich and popular.

Second:

> *When goods increase, they increase who eat them; and what gain has their owner but to see them with his eyes? (5:11)*

If you do get rich, you will soon discover that a crowd of parasites will gather around to spend your money for you. You will get nothing out of them but expense.

He develops this even further:

> *Sweet is the sleep of a laborer, whether he eats little or much; but the surfeit of the rich will not let him sleep (5:12).*

Another disadvantage to having money is that you worry about how to take care of your property. You stay awake nights, stewing about how to keep what you have.

There is still a third disadvantage:

> *There is a grievous evil which I have seen under the sun; riches were kept by their owner to his hurt, and those riches were lost in a bad venture; and he is father of a son, but he has nothing in his hand (5:13-14).*

You can lose riches too. They can disappear over-night. A turn of the wheel, a drop in the Dow Jones Average, and your fortune is gone. Your family may well suffer with you.

Finally, riches will not survive death, but you will:

> *As he came from his mother's womb he shall go again, naked as he came, and shall take nothing for his toil, which he may carry away in his hand. This also is a grievous evil: just as he came, so shall*

> *he go; and what gain has he that he toiled for the*
> *wind, and spent all his days in darkness and*
> *grief, in much vexation and sickness and resent-*
> *ment? (5:15-17)*

You can take absolutely nothing away with you. Life is empty and meaningless for so many wealthy people. They suffer from "Destination Sickness." Having arrived at where they always wanted to be, and having everything they always wanted to have, they do not want anything they've got. And at last they must give it all up.

So the Searcher clearly reveals where the answers to life's quest will be found: It will be in "the house of God," the place where the people of God assemble and the word of God is unfolded. If one listens carefully and does not play dishonest games with God, he will learn to value government and distrust riches.

The Searcher closes the chapter with a return to his repeated theme:

> *Behold, what I have seen to be good and to be*
> *fitting is to eat and drink and find enjoyment in*
> *all the toil with which one toils under the sun the*
> *few days of his life which God has given him, for*
> *this is his lot. Every man also to whom God has*
> *given wealth and possessions and power to enjoy*
> *them, and to accept his lot and find enjoyment in*
> *his toil— this is the gift of God (5:18-19).*

Enjoyment does not come from possessions or from riches. Nor does it come from companionship, from popularity and fame, from the approval and the admiration of others. Enjoyment comes by knowing the Living God and taking everything from his hand with thanksgiving, whether pain or pleasure. That is the gift of God, and that is the lesson of this great book.

Notice how the chapter closes:

> *For he will not much remember the days of his life because God keeps him occupied with joy in his heart (5:20).*

Have you ever met people like that? They have lived a full life, but they seldom talk about the past. Some people live only in the past. William Randolph Hearst, who amassed one of the great fortunes of our time, ended his days amidst all the opulence and splendor of the castle which he built in Southern California, sitting in a basement, playing over and over again the movies of his paramour from Hollywood, in an vain effort to gain a degree of enjoyment from the past. When people discover the richness of life which God has provided, they do not much think of the past, or even talk about it. They do not talk about the future either, because they are so richly involved with savoring life right now.

How good it is to know the Living God, to know that he controls what comes into your life. He expects you to make choices; Scripture always encourages that. But rejoice in the wisdom of a Father's heart, and richly enjoy what is handed you day-by-day. That is the secret of life.

Such a one "will not much remember the days of his life because God keeps him occupied with joy in his heart."

# 5
# THINGS ARE NOT WHAT THEY SEEM

Just when everything seems to be going smoothly, the world can turn sour. That goes for a nation's economic climate, too. Just a few years ago, the economic news in this country was bad (to put it mildly). We faced the possibility of a tremendous recession. In some places it was described as a return to the Great Depression. Unemployment reached record levels in many parts of America.

But the situation is improved today. Economic news is generally much brighter as I sit at my desk writing this chapter—but it may change again by the time this book is published. The pendulum might swing back the other way. Recession might again be knocking at—or knocking down—the door. Unemployment could again skyrocket. The truth is, we must all face the hard times that will surely come. And that makes everyone's heart sink a little; we react emotionally to such bleak circumstances.

Our view of life may be so distorted that we will not be able to see that hard times can become the best years of our lives. That is what the Searcher tells us in Ecclesiastes chapter 6, where he declares that things are not what they sometimes seem to be. We think life is one way but it turns out to be something quite different. We may read everything that happens to us in entirely the wrong way.

The Searcher explains that prosperity may not always be good; and in the first fourteen verses of chapter 7 he takes up the opposite truth, that adversity may not always be bad. What we need, of course, is a true view of good and evil. How may we recognize good when it is good? How may we identify evil for what it is? We would save ourselves much heartache if we could do that . . . and the wonderful thing about Scripture is that it does it. Here we have the true view of good and evil.

There are, first, four statements about prosperity that show us material wealth and abundance are not always good. Here is the first one:

> *There is an evil which I have seen under the sun, and it lies heavy upon men; a man to whom God gives wealth, possessions, and honor, so that he lacks nothing of all that he desires, yet God does not give him power to enjoy them, but a stranger enjoys them. This is vanity; it is sore affliction (6:1-2).*

Immediately Solomon recognizes that one can have abundance of possessions—all that money can buy—

and yet lack the power to enjoy them. It's a heavy burden to bear. Many people today suffer from this. They drive shiny new cars, they have the latest electronic equipment in their luxurious homes, they visit the most fashionable clubs and restaurants. They are trying desperately to enjoy these things—yet their faces have a hollowness about them. Their eyes betray an emptiness inside.

Occasionally I have stepped into casinos in Reno or Las Vegas to see what the places looked like. There I saw people intent on getting rich, desperate to enjoy life more. Yet they looked like death warmed over. They sat there unsmiling, pulling at those one-armed bandits. There was nothing about them to suggest they really *enjoyed* anything they were doing. It looked instead like deadly serious work. What a boring thing that is! I marvel at the jaded lives of those who have everything . . . but who cannot enjoy anything they have.

The Searcher goes on to say that material wealth and abundance can be frustrating when you see a stranger enjoying what you cannot. Can there be anything more irritating than getting what you have always wanted, only to discover that it has lost its luster; then passing it on to someone who cannot afford it but who has a ball with it? That would make one frustrated and resentful: "Why couldn't I enjoy it?"

The key to all this is in the phrase, "God does not give him power to enjoy." This book pounds home that lesson over and over again. Enjoyment does not come with increased possessions—it is a gift which God must give! If he withholds it, no amount of effort can gain it. That is a difficult lesson for some to learn. We are constantly bombarded with alluring pictures in catalogs and in commercials that shout at us the opposite message. Enjoyment, however, is a *gift* from God.

But why would God withhold enjoyment? Why would he not give the power to enjoy if he gives the ability to have? The answer is given in this book. It is clearly stated in chapter 2, verses 25 and 26, where the Searcher says,

> . . . *for apart from him who can eat or who can have enjoyment? For to the man who pleases him God gives wisdom and knowledge and joy* . . .

"To the man who pleases him." Again, I am afraid many read that as though it meant some level of religious performance, some standard of morality like joining a church or coming to meetings. We must understand that the Scriptures never say that. *Faith* is what pleases God! Believing him, taking him at his word and acting upon that word is what pleases God. It is obedience based upon faith. To such a man or woman God gives the gift of enjoying whatever he or she has.

How little or much it may be, it is enjoyed only as a gift poured out from God's hand. That is why gratitude, to be grateful for what you get, is the most important element of our lives.

How contrary this is to the spirit of our age! Shouted at us on every side is the philosophy that we have a right to things. Television commercials constantly tell us this. They hold up some alluring object and accompany it with propaganda that says, "You deserve this. You've got it coming to you. If you were being treated rightly this is what you would have." That is the spirit of the times. Do we realize how it contradicts what the Bible teaches about our relationship to God? How can we be grateful if we only get what we deserve? We cannot be grateful for that. Gratitude only comes when we believe we have been given something we have not earned.

All through Scripture we are told that the proper response of a believer to God is to give thanks for everything: "In everything give thanks, for this is the will of God concerning you" (1 Thessalonians 5:18). This book of wisdom exhorts us to receive everything with a grateful heart, realizing that we do not have it coming to us; it is a gift of God. Even if it is painful for the moment, a wise Father has chosen it for us, and it will yield to us great and rich benefits. You can be as grateful for the pain as for the pleasure. That is the lesson of this book.

The Searcher's second observation is that long life and a big family, without the gift of enjoyment, is a grievous and hurtful thing.

> *If a man begets a hundred children and lives many years, so that the days of his years are many, but he does not enjoy life's good things, and also has no burial, I say that an untimely birth (a stillborn baby) is better off than he. For it comes into vanity and goes into darkness, and in darkness its name is covered; moreover it has not seen the sun or known anything, yet it finds rest rather than he. Even though he should live a thousand years twice told (two thousand years), yet enjoy no good—do not all go to the one place? (6:3-6).*

Even a big family, which usually brings much cheer, excitement and pleasure to life . . . even a long life with many children and grandchildren . . . will not of itself meet man's deep hunger for contentment. It will still leave him restless, unhappy, involved in quarrels and family strife, leaving the heart unsatisfied. Without the gift of enjoyment nothing will satisfy. Nothing will produce long-lasting joy.

If such is the case, the Searcher says, even a stillborn baby is better off. Why? There are two reasons. First, a stillborn infant has no history to live down: "It comes into vanity and goes into darkness, and in darkness its name is covered." No one knows anything about it, it has no history, so no one can put it down or in any way attack it. Furthermore, while it will not experience trouble, the wealthy man will: "It has not seen the sun or known anything; yet it finds rest rather than he." Even long life, say two thousand years of life, would not help. Both the stillborn baby and the wealthy man who lives a long life without enjoyment end up at the same place; neither finds enjoyment.

The third point the Searcher makes is found in verses 7 through 9:

> *All the toil of man is for his mouth, yet his appetite is not satisfied. For what advantage has the wise man over the fool? And what does the poor man have who knows how to conduct himself before the living? Better is the sight of the eyes than the wandering of desire; this also is vanity and a striving after wind.*

Here he points out how man is incapable of finding joy by his own effort. Hard work will not do it: "All the toil of man is for his mouth." Toil is designed to satisfy man's appetite for pleasure and contentment, but hard work and a desperate drive to satisfy oneself along these lines will never work. It cannot produce lasting pleasure.

But neither will wisdom, or even charm. Of wisdom, he says, "What advantage has the wise man over the fool?" You may be wise in your investments, careful with your money, you may pursue pleasure moderately; but it is still not going to work without the gift of enjoyment. If that is all you have, you are no different than the fool. Even a poor man who learns how to charm others ("who knows how to conduct himself before the living") is still left empty, lonely, and miserable inside.

The reason is given in the closing verses of this chapter.

> *Whatever has come to be has already been named, and it is known what man is, and that he is not able to dispute with one stronger than he (6:10).*

Man is up against the unalterable decree of God. The Searcher tells us God has decreed that enjoyment cannot be found by effort, by cleverness, or by the pursuit of pleasure. Enjoyment must be taken as a gift from God's hand. The decree is as unalterable as the law of gravity. You may not agree with God about it, you may not like it, but there it is; it cannot be changed. You cannot dispute with one stronger than you.

The Searcher points out three things about this. First, God decreed it before man was ever created: "Whatever has come to be has already been named"— even before it happened. God created this strange law of life before man ever appeared on earth.

Second, it was decreed in view of what man is: "It is known what man is." God made us. He knows what we are like, how we function, what will satisfy and what will not. He therefore set up this decree that enjoyment cannot be found by possessing things. Jesus said it plainly: "A man's life does not consist of the abundance of things which he possesses" (Luke 12:15).

Third, the Searcher says it was decreed in spite of what man might try to do. "He is not able to dispute with one stronger than he." How are you going to change the laws of God? Although they may appear very much against us, there is nothing we can do about it.

Arguing about it, he goes on to say, does not help.

*The more words, the more vanity, and what is man the better? (6:11).*

C. S. Lewis said it so well: "To argue with God is to argue with the very power that makes it possible to argue at all." How do you change that?

The Searcher goes on to speak of man's weakness. There are two reasons why this law cannot be changed: first, because God decreed it; and second, because man is so limited.

*For who knows what is good for man while he lives the few days of his vain life, which he passes like a shadow? For who can tell man what will be after him under the sun? (6:12)*

He asks two questions. First, who knows true value in life? Where is the man who understands what is good and what is bad? None of us does, so the Searcher asks, "Who knows what is good for man?" Did you ever wish for something you thought was just right for you, and then when you got it you wished you didn't have it? A high school boy once said to me, "I prayed, 'Lord, if I could just go with that beautiful girl I'd be the happiest boy alive.' Then we got acquainted. We went out a few times together, and I found myself praying, 'Lord, if I could just get rid of this girl I'd be the happiest guy alive!'" "Who knows what is good for man?" Surely we do not.

Then the second question, who knows what is coming in the future? "Who can tell man what will be after him?"

Who knows what the results of our present choices are going to be? Given our limited, narrow vision of what life is—which is true of the smartest and most erudite among us—what business have we got complaining to God about how our life is run? Let us accept that we are not wise enough to know what is good for us, and then let us trust God to choose the elements we need.

If prosperity is not always good, as the Searcher has clearly shown, then it is equally true that adversity is not always bad. Suppose hard times do come? What then? Many good and even great things can come out of them.

In chapter 7 a series of proverbs lists the good things that can happen in affliction. Here is the first one:

> *A good name is better than precious ointment;*
> *and the day of death, than the day of birth (7:1).*

There is a play on words here. The Hebrew word for "name" is *shem*, and the Hebrew word for "ointment" or "perfume" is *shemen*. The Searcher is saying that a good *shem* is better than precious *shemen*. This, of course, refers to perfume, which has the ability to attract others.

The Searcher declares that a good name is truly influential. It is not like perfume, which does not last long (even if it is costly). A good name *endures*. One will pass by many garish-looking restaurants to visit some little hole-in-the-wall that serves good food at a decent price. A good name *attracts*. Even the poorest among us can have a name for integrity, for trustworthiness. Even though you may not be able to afford Chanel No. 5 and other expensive perfumes, yet you can always afford a good name.

Another aspect of adversity is the lesson that sorrow teaches.

> *It is better to go the house of mourning than to go*
> *to the house of feasting; For this is the end of all*
> *men, and the living will lay it to heart (7:2).*

When you are confronted with death you are no
longer dealing with side issues; you are dealing at last
with realities. Death leads to realism. Though it will
bring sorrow, grief and mourning, you set aside the
shallow, ephemeral aspects of life and start to deal
with the facts. On the other hand, feasting can be de-
ceitful and lead to unreal living.

Second, the Searcher says, sorrow leads to gladness.

> *Sorrow is better than laughter, for by sadness of*
> *countenance the heart is made glad (7:3).*

And not only gladness, but wisdom:

> *The heart of the wise is in the house of mourning;*
> *but the heart of fools is in the house of mirth (7:4).*

How can that be? How can sorrow, grief, adversity
and pain lead to gladness and wisdom? Anyone who
has been through a painful trial knows that it is often
true.

Even though the events he describes happened a
decade ago, John Ehrlichman's book *Witness To Power*
makes fascinating reading. Ehrlichman served under
Richard Nixon, and thereby was for awhile one of the
most powerful men in the United States. He fell from
power when he became involved in Watergate and
was sent to jail. Here are a few excerpts of his account
before and after the days of Watergate, taken from the
last chapter of his book. He says:

> *When I went to jail, nearly two years after the*
> *cover-up trial, I had a big self-esteem problem. I*
> *was a felon, shorn and scorned, clumping around*

> *in a ragged old army uniform, doing pick and
> shovel work out in the desert. I wondered if anyone
> thought I was worth anything . . . For years I
> had been able to sweep most of my shortcomings and
> failures under the rug and not face them, but dur-
> ing the two long criminal trials I spent my days
> listening to prosecuters tell juries what a bad fellow
> I was. Then at night I'd go back to a hotel room
> and sit alone thinking about what was happening
> to me. During that time I began to take stock.*

He goes on to describe how his marriage failed,
and how he went off by himself, seeking solitude on
the cold and windy shores of Oregon, where he stayed
alone in a cabin:

> *I stayed about two weeks. Every day I read the
> Bible, walked on the beach and sat in front of my
> fireplace thinking and sketching, with no outline
> or agenda. I had no idea where all this was lead-
> ing or what answers I'd find. Most of the time I
> didn't even know what the questions were. I just
> watched and listened. I was wiped out. I had noth-
> ing left that had been of value to me—honor, credi-
> bility, virtue, recognition, profession—nor did I
> have the allegiance of my family. I had managed
> to lose that too . . .*

He moved to New Mexico and started life over in
Sante Fe. Here are the closing words of the book:

> *Since about 1975 I have begun to learn to see
> myself. I care what I perceive about my integrity,
> my capacity to love and be loved, and my essential
> worth. I don't miss Richard Nixon very much, and
> Richard Nixon probably doesn't miss me much
> either. I can understand that. I've made no effort
> to be in touch. We had a professional relationship*

> *that went as sour as a relationship can, and no one*
> *likes to be reminded of bad times. Those interludes,*
> *the Nixon episodes in my life, have ended. In a*
> *paradoxical way, I'm grateful for them. Somehow*
> *I had to see all of that and grow to understand it*
> *in order to arrive at the place where I find myself*
> *now.*

That is a moving confirmation of what the Searcher tells us here! Through times of sorrow and adversity we begin to understand the reality of our lives.

No wonder he immediately adds to this the words of verses 5 and 6:

> *It is better for a man to hear the rebuke of the*
> *wise than to hear the song of fools.*
> *For as the crackling of thorns under a pot, so is*
> *the laughter of the fools; this also is vanity.*

Oftentimes a rebuke will help more than foolish songs and hollow laughter. Adversity can be of much benefit to us.

Still another benefit is found in verses 7 through 10:

> *Surely oppression makes the wise man foolish,*
> *and a bribe corrupts the mind (7:7).*

Here he deals with specific adversity. If you suffer injustice, if someone oppresses you, or if someone bribes another to attack you, that is hard to bear. You want to strike back. But wait, he says:

> *Better is the end of a thing than its beginning;*
> *and the patient in spirit is better than the proud in*
> *spirit.*
> *Be not quick to anger, for anger lodges in the*
> *bosom of fools (7:8-9).*

Nothing has been more of a problem in my life than a short fuse, a quick burst of anger. To learn patience is one of the great lessons that adversity can teach us.

Then he adds to that,

> *Say not, "Why were the former days better than these?" For it is not from wisdom that you ask this (7:10).*

Looking back, it all looks so good, but living through those times wasn't any better than your life now. In fact, ten years from now you will look back on today as the good old days, so remember what they were really like. Time dims our memories of the past so that the present looks bleak—but it is not really so.

Finally he speaks about wisdom:

> *Wisdom is good with an inheritance, an advantage to those who see the sun (7:11).*

If you learn to be wise and thoughtful about life, it has advantages for you.

He continues:

> *For the protection of wisdom is like the protection of money (it can spare you a lot of problems); and the advantage of knowledge is that wisdom preserves the life of him who has it (7:12).*

Out of adversity can come wisdom, and that has great advantages as a protection against further trouble and pain.

But now he comes back to his conclusion:

> *Consider the work of God: who can make straight what he has made crooked? (7:13)*

Under the idea of "crookedness" come all those things we call adversities—pain, injustice, mistreatment, poverty, sickness, accidents. His question is, "Who can straighten what God has made crooked?" God did all this, as he goes on to say clearly in verse 14:

> *In the day of prosperity be joyful, and in the day of adversity consider: God has made the one as well as the other.*

Prosperity and adversity both come from God's hands; a wise Father's heart has given them to you. Let us live by the words of the old hymn,

> *Day by day and with each passing moment,*
> *Strength I find to meet my trials here;*
> *Trusting in my Father's wise bestowment,*
> *I've no cause for worry or for fear.*

God has given all these experiences to us. We must learn to accept and understand that God has chosen them out of love and wisdom. They have a special purpose, stated in these last words:

> *God has made the one as well as the other, so that man may not find out anything that will be after him (7:14).*

God has designed life to be full of the unexpected so we might realize that we do not control our future.

We are not in charge of life. The great Satanic lie that subtly comes at us a thousand times a day is that we are gods, we are in charge, we can plan, we can direct, we can control. In the freedom of will that God has granted us there is enough truth in that so that we easily believe we can ultimately control everything. But the lesson of Scripture, driven home again and again, is that it is not true. *God* is in charge.

What he sends us is always designed to benefit. Even though adversity may have painful aspects, we must understand that it comes from a loving God, and be grateful for it.

An unknown poet has written:

*When God wants to drill a man,*
*And thrill a man, and skill a man:*
*When God wants to mold a man*
*To play the noblest part,*
*When he yearns with all his heart*
*To create so great and bold a man*
*That all the world shall be amazed,*
*Watch his methods, watch his ways—*

*How he ruthlessly perfects*
*Whom he royally elects.*
*How he hammers him and hurts him,*
*And with mighty blows, converts him*
*Into trial shapes of clay*
*Which only God understands.*

*While his tortured heart is crying,*
*And he lifts beseeching hands.*
*How he bends but never breaks*
*When his good he undertakes.*
*How he uses whom he chooses,*
*And with every purpose, fuses him,*
*By every act, induces him*
*To try his splendor out,*
*God knows what he's about!*

# 6
# WHOEVER SAID LIFE WAS FAIR?

The book of Ecclesiastes is the most exhaustive investigation ever made of the value and profit of various lifestyles. Remember that the Searcher is King Solomon, who records for us a faithful, objective and relevant report of what he found in an extensive search which took years of his life. By the middle of the seventh chapter, to which we come now, he can say, "I have seen everything." In fact, he opens this section with those very words.

*In my vain life I have seen everything; there is a righteous man who perishes in his righteousness, and there is a wicked man who prolongs his life in his evil-doing (7:15).*

This central section of Ecclesiastes reveals how to realistically evaluate life. We have seen already that prosperity is not always good; to be wealthy and materially well off is by no means the answer to the hunger of the human heart. We have also seen the corollary truth, that adversity is not always bad. Some of our best times happen when we do not have much, when things are tough.

In this section we learn still another accompanying truth, that the "righteous" are not always righteous. This section declares two great things: that in the real world there is much phony righteousness; and that true wisdom is therefore hard to find.

In verse 15, the Searcher says that one cannot tell the righteous by the fact that they live a long time. In other words, as the proverb has it, "The good often die young." The wicked can live to a ripe old age. There is such a thing as a dirty old man! He does exist, and the bumper sticker tells us that he needs love like the rest of us.

Verses 16 through 19, where this truth is developed, is a greatly misunderstood passage.

> *Be not righteous overmuch, and do not make yourself overwise; why should you destroy yourself? Be not wicked overmuch, neither be a fool; why should you die before your time? It is good that you should take hold of this, and from that withhold not your hand; for he who fears God shall come forth from them all. Wisdom gives strength to the wise man more than ten rulers that are in a city.*

That must be the favorite scripture of many, because it seems to advocate moderation in both good and evil. The Searcher appears to be saying, "Do not be too righteous, and do not be too wicked either, but a little of both does not hurt."

We have all heard people say, "Religion is all right in its place, but don't let it interfere with your pleasure." Moderation in all things is the popular way to go.

But in trying to understand this, we must notice very carefully what the Searcher is saying. The second verb of verse 16, "Do not make yourself overwise," is the key to understanding the verse. In grammar this is called a reflexive verb; that is why the word "yourself" is included. What the Searcher is really saying is, "Do not be wise to yourself; do not be wise in your own eyes, in regard to your own righteousness."

This is a warning against self-righteousness, and properly so. Self-righteous people regard themselves as righteous because they do not do certain things. That, in my judgment, is the major curse of the church today. The New Testament calls it Phariseeism; the Searcher rightly labels it wickedness.

In the book of Job we learn that wickedness is expressed not only by murder, thievery and sexual misconduct, but also by bigotry, racism, pompousness, cold disdain; by critical, judgmental attitudes, by harsh, sarcastic words, by vengeful and vindictive actions. The evangelical prig, male or female, is also a wicked person!

Not only is self-righteousness wicked, but the opposite extreme is wicked too, the Searcher says. The foolish casting off of moral restraints, the abandonment of self-discipline and going in for wild and unrestrained living, is also wickedness.

Furthermore, each of these lifestyles is mutually self-destructive; they result in the same thing. "Why should you destroy yourself?" he asks the self-righteous; "Why should you die before your time?" he says to the self-indulgent. In either case they destroy something of their humanity. This may be true even physically. The self-indulgent may die in a drunken brawl or in a car accident, while the self-righteous will probably die of ulcers, or a heart attack, or as a result of soft, indulgent living.

The proper attitude toward life is found in verse 18:

> *It is good that you should take hold of this (true righteousness) and from that (the wickedness of the world in which we live) withhold not your hand; for he who fears God shall come forth from them all.*

That is the consistent position of the Scripture, Old and New Testament alike. We are not to withdraw from the world in an attempt to escape its evil; we are not to gather our robes of righteousness about ourselves and look down our noses with disdain at those who live morally unrighteous lives. It is good to take hold of true righteousness, but is also good to not withhold oneself from the world. Be out in it, live in it, be in touch with it. Do not seek to avoid it, to hide in a spiritual cocoon, but neither go along with its unrighteous and hurtful attitudes and practices.

The godly way to live, of course, is "He who fears God shall come forth from them all." We have seen this phrase, "The man who fears God," many times in this book. "To fear God" is a full-orbed truth. It means not only to respect God, but to acknowledge his presence in your life; acknowledge him not merely at the end of your life someday, but now. To fear God is to know that he sees all that you do, and that it is his hand that sends circumstances into your life.

The knowledge of God's power, wisdom and love, his willingness to accept you, to change you, to forgive you, to restore you and to stand by you, are all part of fearing God. "To fear God" is to know how to live in the midst of the world and yet not be self-righteous, priggish, smug and complacent. That kind of wisdom "gives strength to the wise man more than ten rulers that are in a city." It is better to learn to live that way than to have ten influential friends in high places who can bail you out when things go wrong!

Solomon now sets forth the truth that we live in a fallen world. There is no righteousness, apart from the gift of God. All have been infected by the virus of evil, he declares in verses 20 through 22:

> *Surely there is not a righteous man on earth who does good and never sins (7:20).*

Do not add "except me" to that statement. The Scripture states this over and over. The Searcher goes on to tell us how we will know the truth of this:

> *Do not give heed to all the things that men say, lest you hear your servant cursing you; your heart knows that many times you have yourself cursed others (7:21,22).*

The unchanging position of Scripture is, as Paul declares in Romans, "All have sinned and fall short of the glory of God." Isaiah puts it this way: "All we like sheep have gone astray; we have turned every one to his own way." In the honesty of our hearts we know that. We can hear it in others if we listen to what people say when they are angry, frustrated, or upset about something. Listen to what Christians mutter under their breath when they are caught in traffic! The Searcher says, "Don't take it too seriously. It is not a personal reaction so much as a revelation of universal evil."

All of us live in a fallen world. We all struggle with a fallen nature which will show itself at any possible moment of weakness, frustration, or anger. That is why, if you hear your servant cursing you, you must realize that he is suffering from the same problem as you do. Do not take it so seriously that you get upset and threaten to fire him, but remember that you are in the same boat. In fact, the Searcher invites you to remember that in your own heart you have done the same thing many times. How refreshingly honest the Scriptures are! They confront us with reality about life.

Because there is none righteous on the earth, the Searcher concludes, true, godly wisdom is very hard to find. He looked for it:

> *All this I have tested by wisdom; I said, "I will be wise"; but it was far from me. That which is, is far off, and deep, very deep; who can find it out? I turned my mind to know and to search out and to seek wisdom and the sum of things, and to know the wickedness of folly and the foolishness which is madness (7:23-25).*

We have seen before how he described the long search that he undertook to investigate all philosophies, seeking to discover the secret of life. He says here that he sought it in himself first of all. Remember that this was written by King Solomon, who was noted in his own time as the wisest man in the world. With that reputation for wisdom he sought in his own life to find the secret. As he puts it here, "I said, 'I will be wise,' but it was far from me." What an honest confession! He found himself short-changed, unable to understand himself.

There is probably no one thing that we are more confident of than this notion that we know ourselves.

How many times have you heard someone say, "No one understands me"? The clear implication is, "I alone understand me." The revelation of Scripture, however, is that if there is one person in this world you do not know, it is you. You do not understand yourself.

We will be puzzled and confused if we try to solve the riddles of life by thinking we understand ourselves. "That which is, is far off and deep, very deep, who can find it out?" asks Solomon. He realizes that the issue lies deep within himself. To try to understand yourself is very difficult. It is like a man trying to look at his own face without using a mirror. The Searcher found it impossible to solve the riddles of his feelings because he did not understand himself.

He goes on to tell us that as he sought, he realized that what he was looking for was the explanation of the mystery of evil. Have you ever wrestled with that? Have you ever asked yourself after you had done something, "Why did I do that? I knew it was wrong, I knew it would hurt somebody, why did I say that?" You were wrestling with the same problem the Searcher faced, that great question of the mystery of evil. The Searcher says he did not find the answer by wisdom, by trying to reason it out.

What he did find was very revealing. The first thing he discovered was what most of us find when we seek the key to our life apart from God—bitterness and death:

> *And I found more bitter than death the woman whose heart is snares and nets, and whose hands are fetters; he who pleases God escapes her, but the sinner is taken by her. Behold, this is what I found, says the Searcher, adding one thing to another to find the sum, which my mind has sought*

*repeatedly, but I have not found. One man among
a thousand I found, but a woman among all these
I have not found. Behold, this alone I found, that
God made man upright, but they have sought out
many devices (7:26-29).*

This is a remarkable revelation of what a keenly intelligent and very resourceful man found out about life. Solomon is honestly recording his own experience.

He found two things. First, he found that he was easily trapped by sexual seduction. He went looking for love. Many a man or woman can echo what he is saying. He went looking for love, and thought he would find it in a relationship with a woman. He went looking for that which would support him, strengthen him and make him feel life was worth the living, but what he found was nothing but a fleeting sexual thrill. He found himself involved with a woman who did not give him what he was looking for at all; he still felt the same empty loneliness as before.

A young woman told me that she sought the answer to the hungers of her life in one relationship after another with men. She said she woke up one morning lying in bed with a man she had met the night before. As she looked at this male sleeping beside her, she felt the most intense loneliness she had ever experienced. She realized then that sex was *compounding*, not solving, the emptiness and loneliness of her life! She went on to tell of finding a relationship with God through the Lord Jesus and testified to the fullness she found in that relationship.

The Searcher also honestly records the way of escape: "He who pleases God escapes her, but the sinner is taken by her." We must remember that this is the man who had seven hundred wives and three hundred concubines; he was involved sexually with one thousand women! In all that experience, sexual athlete that he was, he found nothing to satisfy the searchings of his heart.

But he did come to realize that the man who fears God, who understands God, whose eyes are opened and whose heart is taught by the Word of God, will escape this. In the first nine chapters of Proverbs, which Solomon also wrote, he passes on his experience along this line to young men to show them how to escape this emptiness.

Not only did he find himself trapped by sexual seductiveness, but he says he was also puzzled by a strange observation, recorded in verses 27 and 28: "One man among a thousand I found, but a woman among all these I have not found."

We must read this carefully. As he went through life he occasionally found a loyal, trustworthy, godly, wise man who could be a true friend, a man of integrity; but he never found a woman like that. Out of the thousand women he was involved with, he never found one whom he could trust. Why? Surely it was not because Solomon was a male chauvinist pig, as some may perhaps be tempted to think. In chapter 8 of Proverbs he uses a woman to symbolize true, godly wisdom, and in the 31st chapter of Proverbs he holds up a woman as the supreme example of one who lives a life pleasing to God; that chapter is known around the earth for its exaltation of godly womanhood. Solomon was not a woman hater—that was not his problem.

We can understand his honest remarks here when we remember what was going on in his search. His problem was that when he sought to relate to a woman, he was stymied by immediate sexual involvement. That canceled out discovering who the woman really was. That is the explanation for his words here.

Solomon had no such problem with men. He was not gay. When he sought to relate to a man, he could understand him, hear him, and realize what was going on inside since he was unhindered by any sexual barriers. But not so with a woman.

One of the most important lessons we must learn about life is that sex outside of marriage arrests the mutual process of discovery. You cannot discover who you are or who another person is when you are involved together in wrongful sex. I have seen this happen many times with young couples who were obviously growing in the Lord. They began to know one another, to love one another, to discover things they liked and disliked—and then suddenly the relationship soured, a weirdness set in. Things went wrong and they began to quarrel and fight. Often it turned out that they had given way to their temptations and had gone into sexual experiences together, thus canceling out every attempt to discover who the other one was.

The Scriptures warn us carefully about pre-marital sex. In marriage, good sex will enhance the discovery process; but without marriage, without its commitment and intimacy, sex derails discovery. This is why the Searcher has to record, "I could find a real man among a thousand, but I never found a woman like that." I am sure there were women like that among those he knew, but he could never find one.

Finally, he sums this all up in verse 29:

> *Behold, this alone I found, that God made man (that is, both male and female) upright, but they have sought out many devices.*

The trouble of this world is not with God, but man. Because we will not heed the wisdom of God in the Word of God, we seek to circumvent what he is telling us and try to find the richness of life despite (or apart from) the rules of life that he has set forth. It cannot be done. The inevitable discovery of an honest search is that true life can never be found except where God says it is found—in a relationship with him.

So the Searcher concludes this section, in verse 1 of chapter 8, with a statement of the value of true, godly wisdom. Here is another of those misplaced chapter divisions. We ought to read this as the closing part of chapter 7:

> *Who is like the wise man? And who knows the interpretation of a thing? A man's wisdom makes his face shine, and the hardness of his countenance is changed.*

That is a marvelous, fourfold description of what happens to one who discovers the true wisdom of righteousness as a gift from God, one who walks with God in the fear of God.

First, it will make that person a unique human being: "Who is like the wise man?" One of the follies of life is to try to imitate somebody else. The media constantly bombard us with subtle invitations to look like, dress like, or talk like some popular idol. If you succeed in that, of course, you will be nothing but a cheap imitation of another person. The glory of the good news is that when you become a new creature in Jesus Christ, you will be unique. There will be no one else like you. You will become more and more like Christ, but unlike everyone else in personality. You will be uniquely yourself. You will not be a copy, a cheap imitation, but an original from the Spirit of God. That is the first and most wonderful thing about the wisdom of redemption.

Second, the Searcher says, godly wisdom will give you a secret knowledge: "Who knows the interpretation of a thing?" The implication of that is that the wise man knows. This is what Paul declares in 1 Corinthians 2: "He that is spiritual judges all things." The spiritual man is in a position to pass moral judgment on the value of everything, not because he is so smart, but because the God who teaches him is wise.

Third, such a man will have visible joy: "A man's wisdom makes his face shine." Grace is what makes the face shine, not grease. Grease is what they put in cosmetics to make the face shine or to take away the shine (as the case may be), but it is grace that does it from within. Grace makes the face shine because it is joy visibly expressed on the human face.

Finally, it changes the very inner disposition of a person: "The hardness of his countenance is changed." Have you ever watched somebody under the impact of the Spirit of God soften, mellow and grow easier to live with? That is the work of the Spirit of God.

I could illustrate that with a thousand lives, but I choose to do so with a famous Christian of some generations ago. All of us, whether we know it or not, have sung the hymns of John Newton. One of our favorite hymns was written by him, "Amazing grace! How sweet the sound—that saved a wretch like me!" That is John Newton's story.

He was raised by a godly mother who prayed for him all his life. As soon as he came of age, he joined the slave trade, running slaves from Africa to England. He fell into wild, unbridled living, participating in drunken brawls. At last he ended up, as he himself confesses, "a slave of slaves." He actually served some escaped slaves on the African coast, wretched, miserable and hardly alive. Then he found voyage on a ship back to England. In the midst of a terrible storm in the Atlantic, fearing for his life, he was converted; he remembered his mother's prayers, and he came to Christ. One of his hymns is his own testimony:

> *In evil long I took delight, unawed by shame or fear,*
> *Until a new object met my sight, and stopped my wild career.*
> *I saw One hanging on a tree in agony and blood,*
> *Who fixed his languid eyes on me as near his cross I stood.*
> *Sure, never till my latest breath shall I forget that look.*
> *It seemed to charge me with his death, though not a word he spoke,*
> *A second look he gave, which said, "I freely all forgive;*
> *My blood was for thy ransom paid, I died that thou mayest live."*

And live he did! He became one of the great Christians of England, the author of many hymns in which he sought to set forth the joy, the radiance, the gladness of his life as he found it in Jesus Christ.

This passage of Ecclesiastes should help us understand afresh that what we regard oftentimes as the restrictions and limitations of life which God sets before us are not designed to keep us from joy. Joy is God's purpose for us. These apparent restrictions are designed to guard it so that we find it in the right way and at the right time. Then life will start to unfold in fullness and gladness before us.

Here the Searcher has clearly declared what he emphasizes throughout the whole book of Ecclesiastes: That it is the man or woman who finds the Living God who discovers the answer to the riddles of life.

# 7
# CAN WE TRUST GOVERNMENT?

Chapter 8 of the Book of Ecclesiastes deals directly with an event that recurs periodically in the life of a nation, including ours—the state's right to draft young men for war. It may come as a surprise to learn that this ancient book deals with that problem, but it does. As we look at the passage we hope to get some light on who is right, those who say, "Hell no! We won't go," or those who say, "It's not wacky to wear khaki!"

The Searcher comments on this in a section which considers how we may rightly view good and evil. We have already seen that prosperity is not always good, nor is adversity always evil. In chapter 7 we saw that despite the phony righteousness which abounds in today's religious circles, true wisdom can be found.

But in chapter 8, beginning with verse 2, we will see that despite injustice in government, there *are* proper powers which government wields. Many will recognize immediately that this squares with the apostle Paul's word in Romans 13 about the powers of government. It would be useful to compare that parallel passage with this.

> *Keep the king's command, and because of your sacred oath be not dismayed; go from his presence, do not delay when the matter is unpleasant, for he does whatever he pleases. For the word of the king is supreme, and who may say to him, "What are you doing?" He who obeys a command will meet no harm, and the mind of a wise man will know the time and way (8:2-5).*

In this remarkable passage King Solomon himself, Israel's head of state, teaches us three great scriptural reasons why we should obey government. The first is set forth in verse 2—obey because you are a citizen of that government. This is what is meant by, "because of your sacred oath." Every citizen of the United States has taken, in some form or another, an oath of allegiance to support the government of the United States. If you are a naturalized citizen, you formally took an oath like that when you became a citizen. If you are a natural-born citizen, as most of us are, you restated that oath whenever you said the Pledge of Allegiance:

> *I pledge allegiance to the flag of the United States of America and to the Republic for which it stands . . .*

One translation renders Solomon's words, "Keep the king's command as though it were an oath unto

God." This underscores the seriousness of citizenship. Because we share the blessings of government, we are also responsible to obey the proper powers and laws of that government.

There is a clear suggestion here that such obedience will not always be pleasant. Verse 2 says "because of your sacred oath be not dismayed." That is, there will be times when obeying the government will not be convenient, when it will interfere with other things you want to do. To be summoned for jury duty just when you are leaving for vacation is not at all convenient. To be hit with a zoning restriction that prohibits you from making a desired change on your property is not very pleasant; nor is paying your taxes when they seem a heavy burden. But it is part of a believer's response to government.

Obedience is not based upon convenience; rather, we owe it because, as Paul says in Romans 13, "government is ordained of God." Granted, sometimes this can be unpleasant. At times we can all agree with Will Rogers, "We ought to be grateful that we don't get as much government as we've paid for!" Nevertheless, the place and principle of government is clearly established in Scripture.

A second reason to obey government appears in verses 3 and 4. We should obey because the state has power to compel us to do so.

> *Go from his (the king's) presence, do not delay when the matter is unpleasant, for he does whatever he pleases. For the word of the king is supreme, and who may say to him, "What are you doing?"*

We do not have a king in the United States, but we do have a head of state. He represents the power and the authority of government, down to the lowest elected official. This passage recognizes that the government does have the right of force. Again, Paul reflects this in Romans 13: the government "does not bear the sword in vain." The state has a right to use force.

No more eloquent statements of this right have ever been made than those contained in the Constitution of the United States and the Declaration of Independence. Do you remember how the Constitution begins?

> *We, the people of the United States, in order to form a more perfect union, establish Justice, insure domestic tranquillity, provide for the common defense, promote the general welfare, and secure the blessings of liberty to ourselves and our posterity, do ordain and establish this Constitution for the United States of America.*

To obtain these rights there exist courts, police forces, and armies. The closing words of the Declaration of Independence are also concerned to spell out the powers and function of government:

> *. . . and that, as free and independent states, they have full power to levy war, conclude peace, contract alliances, establish commerce, and to do all other acts and things which independent states may of right do. And, for the support of this declaration, with a firm reliance on the protection of Divine Providence, we mutually pledge to each other our lives, our fortunes, and our sacred honor.*

Thus our Founding Fathers recognized what the Scriptures so clearly state, that government is ordained of God: it has power to function as such, and the citizen is responsible to obey, not only because of his oath of allegiance, but also because the government has power to compel.

The third reason flows out of that:

*He who obeys a command will meet no harm.*
*and the mind of a wise man will know the time*
*and way (8:5).*

It is a wise thing to obey the government. Obedience is expected of everyone. But should someone disregard their responsibility, government has the right to increase punishment until compliance is obtained. A friend of mine recently got a ticket for speeding. She ignored it, thinking that the matter would never come up again.

The original fine for speeding was $25. But because she ignored it, some months later she got an additional notice saying that the fine had advanced to $145—with the clear implication that the longer she waited, the larger the fine would grow.

That is what this verse means by "He who obeys a command will meet no harm." My friend learned a very necessary lesson: the government has power to compel, and the way to escape harrassment is to obey the government and pay the fine. Obedience to the state, the Searcher says, is required as unto God.

What is left up to us is the time and the way. He develops that in verses 5 and 6:

*. . . the mind of a wise man will know the time*
*and way. For every matter has its time and way,*
*although man's trouble lies heavy upon him.*

That takes us back to that wonderful passage in chapter 3, where we learned there is a time and a place for everything, that in God's great plan there is provision made for sorrow and for rejoicing, for tears and for laughter, for war and for peace. Here we are reminded that: "Every matter has its time and its way."

Still, we are given certain freedom regarding the

time and the way we obey. The words, "man's trouble," seem to suggest that it is not always easy to know how or when to obey. Many factors influence that, especially in circumstances like the draft. When and how should this be carried out? Many young men have asked themselves that question.

But even the fact that it is difficult to decide is part of God's program. As believers, we ought to understand that it is not always easy to know what God wants. He does not want it to be easy. We are not robots, given orders to go here or there, having no choice at all. God clearly does not want those kinds of sons and daughters—he tells us that! Yet that is what we ask for when we say to God, "Show me what you want me to do and I'll do it." In other words, "Compel me: give me orders and I'll carry them out." God does not do that. We often struggle, evaluate, weigh, think and puzzle over what we should do— and God wants it that way. That is part of his plan.

Still, the time is not always left up to us. Sometimes the law requires a certain time schedule. If you have to register for the draft, you must do it in a certain length of time; if you have to pay your taxes, you have a certain deadline. But the Searcher says that a way can be found by "the wise man." Though it is not wrong to take advantage of provisions for hardship release—such as might be included in a draft law— nevertheless, the way to obey can be found in every circumstance if we walk in the wisdom of God.

Something else which influences us is found in verse 7:

> *For he does not know what is to be, for who can tell him how it will be?*

The result of obedience to government is uncertain. We do not always know what God intends to work out through our obedience; that is why it is not left up to us to decide whether we ought to obey. God may have blessings in store for us that we could not foresee.

As a young man in my twenties during World War II, I was faced with registration for the draft. At the time I was working for the railroad industry, which by its very nature allowed me to be deferred. The industry was essential to the conduct of the war. But as the war went on and I saw that my friends and all other young men of my age were enlisting in the service, I grew more and more uncomfortable with deferment.

Eventually I joined the Navy. Although I was unsure whether I was doing the right thing, I felt I had to join. What I did not know was that my action would open a door which gave me perhaps the greatest opportunity I have ever had to teach the Scriptures to those who were in desperate need. I was stationed at Pearl Harbor, and through that great port there passed from time to time every sailor in the Pacific Fleet. Many of them were Christian young men who had won others to Christ aboard their ships. We had the great opportunity to hold Bible classes with hundreds of sailors involved. And all this opened itself to me because I was a member of the United States Navy myself.

Furthermore, I did not know that at the end of the war I would be granted the GI Bill of Rights, which would give me enough money to pay for seminary training. In fact, the time I had served in the navy provided me with exactly the right amount to go through four years of seminary training—the month that I graduated from seminary the GI Bill ceased for me.

I could not foresee all that, but God did. So it is

possible that unexpected results will follow when we obey what God has set before us.

In verse 8 the Searcher faces a very sticky point: you may lose your life in obeying the government.

> *No man has power to retain the spirit, or authority over the day of death; there is no discharge from war, nor will wickedness deliver those who are given to it.*

That is a remarkable verse. Three things are clearly stated. First, death is wholly in God's hands. He can preserve someone's life through the most terrible bombardment even though hundreds around him may fall. Many a soldier or sailor has asked himself, "Why did *I* survive when all my buddies were killed? What does God have for *me* that he would allow me to live?" I asked that question myself when dear Christian friends went down with their ships in the Pacific in World War II. I have had to say to myself, "Why wasn't I on that ship?" Many a soldier has had to face the fact that God is saying to him, "I want to use your life." God is able to preserve it. The verse clearly states that death is wholly in his hands. No man has the power to retain the spirit when God calls it home. None has authority to choose the day of his death. It is entirely in God's hands. This is one of the great, encouraging things that a Christian facing military service should realize.

The Searcher's second point is that no one is discharged in time of war. War is an all-out effort by a nation to preserve something of integrity and value, and as such it requires the wholehearted commitment of all its citizens. There is no way out.

Only one soldier since the Civil War has been executed in the United States for desertion. Private Slovik, a very likeable young man who had had a rough time all his life, finally found happiness with his new wife. Then came World War II. He was drafted and put into battle. He was so shaken by the experience that he refused to fight, laid down his gun, and ran away. Finally he was arrested and tried for desertion. Everyone involved from the governmental standpoint was anxious to preserve his life. Yet it became clear that to allow him to escape would demoralize the whole system and open the door for thousands of others to refuse to face the demands of battle. It was the unanimous decision of the military court that he should be executed. His life was taken, testimony to what the Scriptures here declare: "there is no discharge from war." When a nation faces a time of danger, it is the duty of every citizen to come to its defense.

Yet the verse goes on to say that this does not justify every kind of military violence: "Nor will wickedness (that is, military violence, wicked disobedience of the laws of life) deliver those who are given to it." A soldier can be as guilty of murder as any private citizen; he can disobey the laws of justice while wearing a uniform and while engaged in combat. This verse recognizes that wicked violence is not justified simply by wearing a uniform.

Many, perhaps, are uncomfortable at this point. You may be asking yourself, "does that mean that government is always right? Don't governments do wrong at times?" The Searcher faces that in this next section.

> All this I observed while applying my mind to all that is done under the sun, while man lords it over man to his hurt (8:9).

He honestly recognizes that there is evil in government: "Man lords it over others to his own hurt."

John Kenneth Galbraith put this very aptly when he said, "Under capitalism, man exploits man; under communism, it is exactly the reverse." Evil is universal.

All governments do evil, but where does the evil come from? He does not mean that government itself is evil. Government comes from God, according to both the Old and New Testaments. Evil in government arises from the evil in fallen man, living in a fallen world. Who of us is free of evil? Who of us can claim absolute innocence for all we do? No one. There is none righteous, the Searcher found, there is no one who does not do evil. There is no government, therefore, that does not have evil within it.

He gives two very flagrant examples of this.

> *Then I saw the wicked buried; they used to go in and out of the holy place, and were praised in the city where they had done such things. This also is vanity (8:10).*

He had been to the funeral of a prominent government leader, a man whom everybody knew was a wretch and a reprobate, even though outwardly he appeared holy and righteous as he went in and out of the temple. But at his funeral he was praised, exalted and glorified. None of his evil deeds was mentioned. That is evil, says the Searcher.

The death a few years ago of Soviet Premier Leonid Brezhnev was a clear example of this. He personally gave the order for the invasion of Afghanistan and for the destruction of millions of innocent people in various parts of the world. But none of this was mentioned at his funeral. Instead he received glowing tributes and was buried as a hero of the Soviet Union. We do not need to point the finger only at Russia— we do the same thing over here. There are many wretches here buried in honorable graves and remembered as great leaders, yet who were wicked and violent men.

We find a second example in verse 11:

> *Because sentence against an evil deed is not executed speedily, the heart of the sons of men is fully set to do evil.*

What an honest, accurate observation on human life! Delays in justice often increase crime and encourage criminals. When justice is delayed or circumvented, when on technicalities judges turn loose criminals who clearly are guilty of outrageous crimes—this only encourages more crime and makes it clear that evil can be present in government.

Nevertheless, the Searcher finds cause for patience in the twofold promise that follows.

> *Though a sinner does evil a hundred times and prolongs his life, yet I know that it will be well with those who fear God, because they fear before him; but it will not be well with the wicked, neither will he prolong his days like a shadow, because he does not fear before God. There is a vanity which takes place on earth, that there are righteous men to whom it happens according to the deeds of the wicked (righteous people treated like they are wicked), and there are wicked men to whom it happens according to the deeds of the righteous (obvious criminals treated as though they were righteous). I said this also is vanity (8:12-14).*

The Searcher clearly admits the evil of this, but two things encourage him. First, God will preserve his own despite what happens to their bodies. Jesus said to his disciples, "Do not fear those who kill the body but cannot kill the soul; rather fear him who can destroy both soul and body in hell" (Matthew 10:28). That is, the claims of God take precedence over the threats of mankind. We are to walk in the light of that. God is able to take care of his own. In God's eyes, what happens to our bodies is not nearly as significant as what happens to us. Those who walk in fear before God (meaning those who love, respect, honor and obey God) will be kept by God, regardless of what happens to their bodies.

Second, God will judge the wrong in his own time. Though the sinner seems to get away with murder, and does the same thing a hundred times, nevertheless God is watching. An accounting will be made. Though the rewards of life sometimes seem reversed—wicked men get what the righteous ought to have, and righteous men get what the wicked deserve—the promise stands that the wicked shall not "prolong his days like a shadow."

*The wicked shall not prolong his days like a shadow*— that's an interesting phrase referring to the wicked man's influence after his death. Life prolonged like a shadow is not real life: it is the influence of a man after his death. It is remarkable that although notoriously wicked men throughout history may have been praised and honored during their lives, they are always revealed at death to have been what they really were—*wicked*. Adolf Hitler and all the Nazis associated with him are now despised and abhorred around the world; they have not been able "to prolong their days like a shadow." God works to bring truth and justice to light.

So the Searcher comes to the same conclusion in verse 15 that he's reached before:

> *And I commend enjoyment, for man has no good thing under the sun but to eat, and drink, and*

*enjoy himself, for this will go with him in his toil
through the days of life which God gives him under
the sun.*

Do not misunderstand! This is not justification for
living it up now, for saying, "Eat, drink and be merry
for tomorrow we die." That philosophy is based upon
a lie, the illusion that enjoyment comes from pleasant
circumstances. If this book teaches us one thing, it
tells us that is not true. Enjoyment does not come
from happy, pleasant circumstances, where everything is going the way we like it. That is what the
world believes. That is what underlies the television
commercials and the magazine ads of our day.

No, according to this book, enjoyment is a gift of
God which can accompany even difficult and hard circumstances. That is why he encourages us to seek it.
True enjoyment, true contentment, does not come
from having everything the way you like it. It comes
no matter what you are going through, as a gift from
the God of glory, who is able to give you peace and
contentment in the midst of the pressures, problems,
and dangers of life.

Surely this is what the apostle Paul meant in
Philippians: "I have learned the secret both how to be
abased and to abound." What secret? He tells us: "I
can do all things through Christ who strengthens
me." The secret of contentment, whether you are
abased or whether you abound, is in the realization
that a Loving Father—the Living God—is working
out strange and inscrutable purposes in your life
which you cannot always guess at or estimate.

Some of you may be going through hard times.
Periodically young men will face things like draft reg-
istration and will become afraid of what will happen.
It is not convenient, it interrupts the affairs of life.

But there are many things like that—accidents can do that, disease can do that. Life must be taken the way it is. The glory of the Scriptures is that they do not try to evade life, to put over it a veil, to doll it up or dress it up to make it look acceptable. Scripture faces life the way it is; but it also tells us that God has provided an answer, and that answer is found by those who walk before him, love him, fear him, trust him and rest their lives in his hands.

This does not excuse us from the struggles of life, or from the need to make decisions. But it does reassure us that those who walk with God will find a source of contentment and satisfaction that is a gift from the Lord of grace.

# 8
# AH, SWEET MYSTERY OF LIFE

One of the songs popular in the early decades of the 20th century was Victor Herbert's *Ah, Sweet Mystery of Life*. It posed the question, "What makes life truly significant?" His solution to the question was human love:

*For it is love for which the world is seeking;*
*and it is love and love alone which can repay.*

But King Solomon, in his quest to understand the riddles of life, does not agree with that. He found that the secret of life is enjoyment, a sense of contentment about life. That is where the answers are found.

This section, beginning with verse 16 of chapter

8, marks the last of the four major divisions of
Ecclesiastes. From here to the end of the book the author does not introduce anything new. He simply repeats and enlarges upon the claim which he has made
all along, that the significance of life is found only in
daily contact with a Living God.

In this section he would remind us that we are to
take life as it comes and not insist on understanding
everything about it. Here he gives four good reasons
for not trying to solve all the problems and answer all
the questions that life throws at us.

The first reason is found in 8:16-17:

> *When I applied my mind to know wisdom, and
> to see the business that is done on earth, how neither
> day nor night one's eyes see sleep; then I saw all the
> work of God, that man cannot find out the work
> that is done under the sun. However much man
> may toil in seeking, he will not find it out; even
> though a wise man claims to know, he cannot find
> it out.*

The Searcher's claim is quite clear. Life is too complicated, too vast, too filled with conflicting elements for anyone to figure out all the answers. Even
sleepless toil will not solve life's mysteries. Though
we stay up all night and day, trying to think through
and understand the complicated events that bring to
pass the circumstances of our lives, we will never fully
understand.

The Bible never condemns our attempts at understanding life. Rather, the pursuit of knowledge is
everywhere encouraged in Scripture. We must never
adopt the attitude of anti-intellectualism that charac-
terizes some segments of Christianity.

The mind *does* matter. We are to reason and think
about what God is doing and what life gives us. But

we must always remember, as the argument makes clear here, that no matter how much we try to understand life, mysteries will still remain. We do not have enough data, nor do we have the ability to see life in its totality, to answer all the questions. We must be content with some degree of mystery.

Though these words were written by the wisest man of the ancient world, a man who had gained a reputation for wisdom, yet he freely admits that man cannot know all the answers. He says that even diligence in labor will not unravel life's mysteries: "However much man may toil in seeking, he will not find it out." We will still be left knitting our brows, scratching our heads, and asking the eternal "Why?"

Men often claim to know the answers behind what happens to us, but they are only deceiving themselves. Many people are unwilling to accept the truth of Scripture until they can understand everything in it. But if you wait for that, you will never make it. This book was written almost 2,500 years ago, yet the truth it represents is so vast that even in our age of advanced knowledge no one can find all the answers.

Today many hope that the computer will solve the great mysteries of life. The hope of humanity today centers around this remarkable invention, with its ability to do far more than a single human mind can comprehend. I am not denigrating the marvel of computer science; it has changed the whole course of our age. But even these great computers, with their ability to compress knowledge into micro-chips containing information which once could only have been found in whole libraries, nevertheless still cannot solve all the problems of life. Life is simply too complicated.

Think about your own life, about how many of the things that have happened to you have been determined by events over which you had no control, and which had to fall together in a certain pattern before they could ever have come to pass.

How, then, *can* we understand that strange merging of simplicity and complexity? The Qoheleth argues that life is too complicated for us ever to answer all the questions and understand all the mysteries. We must learn to cry with the apostle Paul, "O the depth of the riches and wisdom and knowledge of God! How unsearchable are his judgments and how inscrutable his ways!" (Romans 11:33)

The Qoheleth has a second argument, in chapter 9, verse 1, which reflects this word quoted from Paul:

> *But all this I laid to heart, examining it all, how the righteous and the wise and their deeds are in the hand of God; whether it is love or hate man does not know.*

"I have been meditating on this, observing, seeking and thinking about it," he says. "I have come to the conclusion that even though we may understand that we are in the hand of God, nevertheless it is difficult to know from the events that happen to us whether we have his approval or disapproval" (whether it is love or hate).

This has been stated several times already in this book. We saw that prosperity is not always a sign that God is happy with you; even the wicked prosper sometimes. Adversity, on the other hand, is not always a sign that you are being punished by God. The book of Job is proof of that. Job's three tormentors, whom he called his "friends," were convinced that what was happening to Job was a sign that God was angry at him and was punishing him for sin. But by the end of the book it is clear they are entirely wrong. All suffering, all personal problems, do not always

AH, SWEET MYSTERY OF LIFE 117

come (although sometimes they do) as a result of God's disapproval.

So again we must learn to live with mystery. We are not smart enough, we do not see enough, we do not understand enough. None of our vaunted technology will answer all the questions. Eventually we must agree with God's words, "My thoughts are not your thoughts, neither are my ways your ways" (Isaiah 55:8). That is one of the most difficult lessons to learn in life. We think that because God tells us certain things about himself we can figure out what he is going to do.

We must resist that. We can never anticipate God's sovereign plans. "For as the heavens are higher than the earth, so are my ways higher than your ways and my thoughts than your thoughts" (Isaiah 55:9). God will never be false to his character; he will never contradict what he said. We are just not smart enough always to figure it out or anticipate it.

Beginning at this latter part of verse 1 and running through verse 6 is a section in which the Searcher confronts death as the ultimate mystery. This is a rather gloomy section. In reading through this book you may have noted that the author seems preoccupied with death. We are not used to that today. We live in a time when people are busily trying to forget about death. We have devised means by which we can— temporarily at least— maintain the illusion that life is going to go on forever. But the Scriptures are honest and realistic. Consequently they often face the fact of death. We see that in this passage:

> *Everything before them (us) is vanity, since one fate comes to all, to the righteous and the wicked, to the good and the evil, to the clean and the unclean, to him who sacrifices and him who does not*

> *sacrifice. As is the good man, so is the sinner; and he who swears is as he who shuns an oath. This is an evil in all that is done under the sun, that one fate (one event) comes to all; also the hearts of men are full of evil, and madness is in their hearts while they live, and after that they go to the dead (9:1b-3).*

Death is the great equalizer, he says. No matter if we are righteous or unrighteous, good, bad, or indifferent, death comes to all. Death is the great proof that there is something wrong about humanity; it forces us to face reality.

I have often noticed that some people, non-Christians especially, are very uncomfortable at funerals. They are nervous and edgy. They want to get it over quickly and get back to their local bar or their comfortable living room. I have often asked myself, "what is it about funerals that makes people so nervous?"

The answer I came to is that a funeral doesn't permit us to escape ultimate reality. A funeral is proof that we are not in control of our own lives. Few would choose to die if they had any way of preventing it, yet there is going to be an end to our existence. This is what makes people uncomfortable and anxious to get back to the soothing illusions of life.

The fact that death comes to both good and bad forces us to face the evil within us. Notice what this Searcher concludes: "Also the hearts of men are full of evil, and madness is in their hearts while they live" (verse 3b). That is the reason for death. According to the Scriptures, death comes because of sin: "Sin came into the world...and death through sin" (Romans 5:12). Death spread throughout humanity because there is evil in us.

Our own personal death is the hard, square peg that refuses to fit into all the round holes we plan for our future; it is the sand in our oyster that irritates us and makes our spirits protest against it. Why should we learn all these great lessons of life, just to give them all up without opportunity to use them once we finally have them mastered? Something about that makes us protest.

If we have been brought up to believe the universal lie of our day—which is being flung at us all the time through the media—that we deserve to live, then this constantly approaching termination of our life challenges that illusion. In the eyes of the God of the universe, we do not deserve to live. If we are allowed life beyond death it is a gift of God's grace, not something we have earned ourselves. Something in us makes us deserve to die; that is what universal death declares.

That is what makes everybody essentially religious and why man cannot live like an animal. Even those who claim atheism, and who attempt to act and live as though there were no God, demonstrate from time to time that they do not really believe that. Beyond death is something or someone—they do not know who or what—waiting for them. So they cannot be comfortable with the idea of atheism. They have to find answers to the problems of life, and death is what forces them to do that.

An article by Brooks Alexander of the Spiritual Counterfeits Project in Berkeley, makes a marvelous statement about this theme of death.

> *Just as death is, humanly speaking, a final and total separation, so the awareness of that end shatters our attempt to find some sense or value in the pattern of life here and now.*

When people try to live only for this life, when all their values are centered here and they see nothing beyond this, they are never able to solve the riddles or questions of life. The thing that constantly intrudes upon them is the fact of death; they cannot find any final philosophy that comforts and satisfies when they think of death.

Alexander continues:

> *As that final entropy creeps backward into our every experience, it brings with it a conviction of brokenness, anxiety and alienation that penetrates to the heart of our being. All religion ultimately is an attempt to come to terms with the pervasive and insidious fragmentation of our lives that is introduced by the prospective certainty of death.*

Somehow we sense this even though we will not talk about it. We have to try to find an answer, and that is what makes us religious. Alexander concludes,

> *Humanity cannot therefore escape a religious response to its condition, because individual humans can never escape the fact that they must die. This religious response is specifically a groping for some ground of unity that will enable us to grasp an unknown harmony beyond the brittle disintegration of meaning that fractures all our hopes and pleasures.*

Those insightful statements simply mean that we are restless and unhappy until we find an answer beyond ourselves that will give unity to our life both now and in that which may follow. Therefore we become religious beings.

Notice how Qoheleth continues:

> *But he who is joined with all the living has hope (That is, while there's life there's hope), for a liv-*

> *ing dog is better than a dead lion. For the living*
> *know that they will die, but the dead know noth-*
> *ing, and they have no more reward; but the memory*
> *of them is lost. Their love and their hate and their*
> *envy have already perished, and they have no more*
> *for ever any share in all that is done under the sun*
> *(9:4-6).*

This, of course, does not mean there is no life after death. This is clearly written from the perspective of this life, "under the sun." From that perspective, when people die they cannot return; all the glamour, joy, satisfaction, peace and happiness that this life can afford is forever ended. There is no question about that, and that is all this is stating.

So if we are going to get anything out of life, if our present existence is to have any meaning at all, it must be found now; that is his argument. Do not waste your life, do not run after every titillating experience, every empty pleasure that life may fling at you. Do not try to lose yourself in a merry round of forgetfulness. Use life—that is his argument. Fill it to the full, discover its purpose now, for whatever meaning life may have it must be found *right now.*

Thus we are not to seek after comfort, but significance. "What are you living for?" That is his question. It may be put, "What are you dying for? What is the purpose of your existence?" I urge everyone individually to answer that. Why are you here? What is it all about? If life has any purpose at all it must be found in what happens now. And it is this book's goal to bring us to an answer, to help us see what that purpose is.

Once again the Searcher comes to the conclusion— already reached many times already—which is expressed most fully in verses 7-10:

> *Go, eat your bread with enjoyment, and drink*
> *your wine with a merry heart; for God has already*
> *approved what you do. Let your garments be al-*
> *ways white; let not oil be lacking on your head.*
> *Enjoy life with the wife whom you love, all the*
> *days of your vain life which he has given you under*
> *the sun. Whatever your hand finds to do, do it with*
> *your might; for there is no work or thought or*
> *knowledge or wisdom in Sheol, to which you are*
> *going.*

"Sheol" means the grave. It does not, in this reference at least, mean hell. It means the grave, the end
of this life.

In this remarkable verse there is a statement of
what the New Testament calls the New Covenant,
God's new provision for living. It is clear from the
New Testament that God has given a gift of approval,
of righteousness. Because we already have that by
faith, we are freed; no longer do we have to struggle
vainly to please God. We can live in a way that does
please him because we have already been accepted and
approved by him.

Notice how clearly that is stated in verse 7: "Go
and eat your bread with enjoyment, and drink your
wine with a merry heart; for God has already approved what you do." This is a recognition, even in
the Old Testament, of a relationship of righteousness
that has been established. We know now that that
basis was laid in our Lord's coming into this world in
time, and in his subsequent death and resurrection.
Yet it is applied to people in the Old Testament, as
well as in the New, who had faith in what God declared, who believed his word and thus were given the
gift of righteousness.

Here the Searcher declares what is the real basis for

life. If you want to find significance in your life, if you want to find deep meaning, peace and contentment, this is the basis of it: Believe what God has given you already, and then, on that basis, live your life to the full. Fill it with all that is of value, reason and worth.

"Let your garments be always white," says verse 8. White garments are a symbol in Scripture of practical righteousness, of good deeds which flow out of this new relationship.

"Let not oil be lacking on your head." Oil is the symbol of the Holy Spirit at work. So here is a life filled with the Spirit, full of good works, all flowing out of the realization that we are already accepted by God. That is the new basis for living.

That is what Paul describes in Romans: "Sin will have no dominion over you, since you are not under law (with its demand that you measure up before God will accept you), but under grace" (with its marvelous provision of righteousness as a gift, Romans 6:14). It is yours for the taking, though you do not deserve it, and by it you are rendered fully accepted and loved by God.

Right living follows that, and thus Solomon encourages us to live a normal life. "Enjoy life with the wife whom you love, all the days of your life." God likes that. He ordained marriage to make that possible, and it is right to enjoy the fullness of marriage, its companionship, its conjugal joys.

And enjoy your God-given work! Work is not a curse, it is not something we are forced to do in order to keep alive. Work is a God-given blessing. In days of increasing unemployment many rediscover that it is a pleasant thing to have work to do. Do it with all your might; that is the way to enjoy it. Throw yourself into it, do not just get through the best you can so you can get home and start enjoying yourself. The modern proverb says, "The spirit is willing but the flesh is ready for the weekend!" Many of us live (or seek to live) that way, but that is not the biblical way. The biblical approach is that work is given to you as a gift of God, so enjoy it; do it with all your might, because it is God's gift to you.

Do we live like this? We who are Christians, we who have experienced the gift of righteousness and have discovered the secret of contentment, of being able to handle even difficult conditions because of the joy that God imparts to us by his presence within—have we begun to live this way? I ask myself that. Is there an aura of peace about all that I do? When people look into my eyes, do they see a heart at rest, at peace? When they look into yours, do they see that?

Watch the eyes of people who are filling the stores and offices and you will often see emptiness, loneliness, misery and heartache. But Christians are called to a different way of life, to a secret that others do not know. There is to be calmness, a peace, a consciousness about us that no matter what happens, it is never going to be too bad or too difficult, because we have with us a God who will enable us to handle it. Do we view life that way?

What is your view of approaching death? Do you have some sense of anticipation about it, with the awareness that beyond death is the final explanation of all the unanswered questions of life?

I became a Christian when I was 11 years old. Like all young boys, I faced life with mixed feelings of anticipation and dread. But one thing I have always wanted to do was to grow old. God has answered that prayer! Now, as I near the end, I can say that looking ahead is filled with happy anticipation that God is going to answer all the questions which I have had to leave unanswered. The full meaning of this present experience will never be known until death intervenes. Then will come all the answers, abundantly, satisfyingly, fully.

That is the Christian perspective of life. If we succumb to the empty view of the world around us, we too will find ourselves all ajitter, frustrated, bitter, angry, and upset with our circumstances. But these words of Solomon call us to realize that the meaning of life can never be found by trying to solve all its problems. Rather, it is by trusting in the Living God, who knows what he is doing and who is working out his strange purposes through our lives, teaching us all we need to know as we go on through. Then our eyes will reflect the peace of God and our hearts shall respond with joy at the promises that await a fulfillment yet to come.

# 9
# THE ONLY
# WAY TO GO

We have all seen the wall plaque which says, in a strong German accent, "Ve grow too soon oldt, und too late schmart." Many people would agree that age increases faster than wisdom. By the time you learn what you need to know it is already too late to use it!

But in the book of Ecclesiastes we learn that although that is a common experience, it is not a necessary one. It is possible to learn before it is too late the wisdom which will guide you through life.

Wisdom, however, will not help you avoid the hurt and pain of life. Many people make the mistake of thinking that wisdom will deliver them from all pressure and struggle. It will not. We learn in this book that struggle, pain, pressure, and sorrow all are part of the learning process. But by discovering and obeying the wisdom of God, life will not be rendered bitter, angry, or resentful. You will not find yourself plunged into a morass of self pity and depression. You will not find your life ravaged and torn apart, with all your dreams collapsed at your feet.

The wisdom of God will lead you into fullness and liberty and inward peace in the midst of the pressures and dangers of life. That is the message of the book of Ecclesiastes, as it is the message of the whole Bible.

Beginning in chapter 9, verse 11, the Searcher tells us that the first and probably most difficult lesson of all is that natural gifts in themselves are not enough to handle life; natural abilities and diligent effort will not lead us into truly successful living.

> *Again I saw that under the sun the race is not to the swift, nor the battle to the strong, nor bread to the wise, nor riches to the intelligent, nor favor to the men of skill; but time and chance happen to them all. For man does not know his time. Like fish which are taken in an evil net, and like birds which are caught in a snare, so the sons of men are snared at an evil time, when it suddenly falls upon them (9:11-12).*

Many have had experiences that confirm this. All our carefully laid plans have fallen apart; all our hopes that we had what it took to succeed crumbled, and we could not understand why. We had to learn, as this text says, that "the battle is not always to the strong, nor the race to the swift."

That is often true in athletics. In the early part of this century Jim Thorpe won many gold medals at the Olympic Games. He stood before the King of Sweden and was publicly acknowledged as the greatest athlete of his time. Yet all those medals and honors had to be given back when it was learned that as a boy he had played professional baseball for five dollars a season, which rendered him no longer an amateur.

It is not always the strong, the mighty, the able and the gifted who win in politics, either. We have often seen men and women whom everyone thought a cinch to win public office, defeated, unable to fulfill their dreams. "The battle is not always to the strong," though many strong men and women have sought the awards and the prizes of men.

The Nobel Prize was given a few years ago to a little woman in India, Mother Teresa, who ministers to the needs of the poor around her. And though Hollywood does its best to impress the American public, the picture that was named Best Motion Picture of 1982 was *Chariots of Fire*, the story of a Christian athlete. Solomon clearly tells us that natural gifts are never enough in themselves.

Other factors really make the difference. "Time and chance happen to them all." What does he mean by that? We often hear, "You have to be the right person, at the right place, at the right time." There are elements of rightness which must come together before the abilities that someone has may accomplish his desire. What the Searcher is saying, of course, is that life is not really in our control.

The illusion which the secular media presses upon us all the time is that we can arrange life by our choices. "It's your life! You can live it the way you please." So the television commercials proclaim. But Solomon says it cannot be done that way. "Time and chance happen to them all." Just when you think you have something under control it can all fall apart. Disasters come when least expected: "Like fish which are taken in an evil net, and like birds which are

caught in a snare." Everything can suddenly and un-
expectedly disintegrate. Every one of us has had some
experience of that.

But his point is that there is a wisdom which can
handle that, too. Even though disaster may strike, it
can be turned into victory. He gives us an example in
verses 13-16:

> *I have also seen this example of wisdom under
> the sun, and it seemed great to me. There was a
> little city with few men in it; and a great king
> came against it and besieged it, building great
> siegeworks against it. But there was found in it a
> poor wise man, and he by his wisdom delivered the
> city. Yet no one remembered that poor man. But I
> say that wisdom is better than might, though the
> poor man's wisdom is despised, and his words are
> not heeded.*

There is no record of this event elsewhere in Scripture. Perhaps Solomon, the greatest king of his day,
heard this story from a foreign delegation. It may be
that he was confused about an incident, recorded in 2
Samuel chapter 20. When Solomon was still a boy,
King David sent his general, Joab, to capture a
traitor named Sheba, who had taken refuge in a small
city in Northern Israel. Joab set his army around the
city, built siege works against it, and was ready to
knock down the walls and capture the city when a
wise woman called out to him from the walls and
suggested that the leaders of the city throw the
traitor's head out to Joab. They did so, and thus saved
the city. Perhaps that is the event Solomon refers to
here.

In any case, God's wisdom can turn what looks like
sure defeat into victory, although that wisdom may
not even be remembered; it may even be popularly

rejected. That is what verse 16 implies: "I say that wisdom is better than might, though the poor man's wisdom is despised, and his words are not heeded." Popular rejection is no sign that something is wrong or ineffective.

We must remember today that the world will never applaud the basic truths of the Christian faith. Why? Because Christianity judges the world, points out its error and exposes its illusions. It humbles it. The world cannot take that. So we can expect that the wisdom which we learn from God will not necessarily be popular. Nevertheless it is that which can deliver, that which can free.

I have seen in various metropolitan newspapers a full-page ad which had been placed by a Christian group. One paragraph stated:

> *God promised a Messiah, a deliverer, a problem-solver. And if there is anything more difficult than the fact of sin, it's the idea that God solves our problems. But He can! He can make us want peace, give us hearts to care about one another, relieve guilt, mend broken homes, give meaning to our lives and diminish the din of the Twentieth Century with the music of His love.*

That eloquently expresses the message of the Searcher. How humbling it is to lean on the wisdom of God!

What is this wisdom we are talking about? All through this book we have been looking at wisdom versus foolishness, and in the current section there is a great contrast drawn between them. What does the Bible mean when it uses those terms?

It ought to be clear to us by now that true wisdom acts upon the revelation of reality which the Scriptures give us. Wisdom leads to actions that are controlled by the revelation of God. In Romans 12:2 Paul says, "Do not be conformed to this world (do not run after all the attractive, illusive dreams shouted at you constantly by the world), but be transformed by the renewal of your mind."

Think Christianly about life! Look at what you are going through, not from the standpoint of what seems right— the Scriptures everywhere warn about that—but upon what is right, according to the word of God. Here is true wisdom: "Trust in the Lord with all your heart, and lean not on your own understanding. In all your ways acknowledge him, and he will direct your paths" (Proverbs 3:5-6). The opposite, of course, is foolishness, to adopt the secular mind, the spirit of the age, to run after the advice of those devoid of insight from the Word of God.

There follows in this next section a tremendous contrast between wisdom and foolishness, which I would like to illustrate at a very pragmatic level. We recently learned that there are at least twenty-three couples at our church who are either contemplating or actually involved in divorce. That reflects a running after the spirit of the age, the wisdom of the world, rather than following the wisdom of God.

We need to remember what Solomon himself warned us about earlier in this book. In chapter 5 he said, "When you vow a vow to God, do not delay paying it." Married couples have taken sacred vows before God and human witnesses, that they would stay together "for better or for worse" until death shall part them. That is the wisdom of God. That is what preserves a society. If anything can arrest the fragmentation of life around us, this breakdown of morals and all the other terrible things that are happening in our day, it has got to come from Christians who will stand against the spirit of the age, who will refuse to go along with corrupt suggestions on every side.

Solomon goes on to warn, "It is better that you should not vow than that you should vow and not pay. Let not your mouth lead you into sin, and do not say before the messenger (the representative of God) that it was a mistake (that is what many are saying today, "I made a mistake!"); why should God be angry at your voice, and destroy the work of your hands?"

That is not painting God as a killjoy, as a heartless avenger who visits severe judgment upon people. It rather recalls that God has set the rules of life, and he does not change them. To forgive us does not mean he relinquishes the penalty of our misdeeds; it means that he goes through it with us, he strengthens us in the midst of it. But the agony and the hurt is all there.

I want to express the deep sense of sympathy that I personally have, as do all the elders and pastors of our church, with couples who are struggling with their marriages. This is not at all uncommon. Almost all married couples go through pain, hurt, and struggle. I remember how hopeless things looked at times in the early years of my own marriage, how difficult it was to relate to one another, how easy it would have been to walk away, forget the whole thing and start over. But that is why there are marriage vows. They help us face up to a situation that will result in tremendous learning about ourselves.

The problem with every threatened marriage is the people involved in the marriage—both of them! They need to know something about themselves; that is what we have seen from the Scriptures. We do not realize that we are mysteries to ourselves. Conflict in marriage helps us discover what we are contributing to every situation. To flee the marriage is but to flee into another set of problems, hurts, and pains that are usually worse than the ones you are running from. Many testify that the divorce which they thought was so simple a solution to a mistake they felt they had made, only introduced them into a more painful and hurtful situation, and one that continued in many ways for the rest of their lives.

My counsel to those who are struggling in this area is to call off the legal dogs and seek counsel and help from those who are able to help you through these difficult times. Look to the Lord, look to your God, for help in solving the problems of life. That is why Jesus came, to give us hearts to care about one another, to relieve our guilt and to mend our broken homes.

With that situation in mind, let us look at the verses that follow:

> *The words of the wise heard in quiet are better than the shouting of a ruler among fools (9:17).*

That simply says that the insights of Scripture—heard in the inner self, quietly, before God alone—are more effective in solving problems than worldly rhetoric or propaganda, better than the ideas of a prominent opinionmaker who says popular things but which are contrary to Scripture. In the Bible, rulers are not always governors and kings; they are opinionmakers, shapers of the minds of men. Yet what they say is often only what foolish people around them want to hear.

The words of God's wisdom, heard in quiet, are much more effective than such empty propaganda.

He goes on:

> *Wisdom is better than weapons of war, but one sinner destroys much good. Dead flies make a perfumer's ointment give off an evil odor; so a little folly outweighs wisdom and honor (9:18-10:1).*

This first axiom is true of actual battles that nations have fought. Oftentimes quiet, biblical principles have overcome the power of force. Look at the Civil Rights movement under Dr. Martin Luther King, Jr., who based his actions and leadership upon scriptural principles of non-violent protest. That is a vivid example of how powerful such a movement can be in overcoming injustice and outright physical abuse. It can set things right better than can warfare.

This is true in an individual's or in a couples' life as well. Wisdom is better than war, better than fighting.

But a warning is included here: one sinner is like a dead fly in the perfumer's ointment which can give off a foul odor. One person, insisting on following the world's philosophy, can often harm, arrest, or even destroy the healing work of wisdom.

The Searcher says,

> *A wise man's heart inclines him toward the right, but a fool's heart toward the left (why isn't that the motto of the Republican Party?). Even when the fool walks on the road he lacks sense, and he says to everyone that he is a fool (10:2-3).*

God's wisdom provides a safer guide through life than the impulsive actions of those who follow whatever views happen to be popular. Even when a fool does take the right course, he often makes it clear that he does not understand why; he reveals his ignorance when he talks. Dr. Lewis Sperry Chafer used to say at Dallas Seminary, "It is much better to keep silent and let everybody think you are a fool, than to open your mouth and remove all doubt!"

The Searcher is saying that even when fools take the right course and do the right thing, the way they explain or describe it reveals how wrong they are. It is like the man who jumped into the water to save another who was drowning. Asked why he did so, he said, "I had to; he had my watch on!" So even when a fool walks on the road he lacks sense, and says to everyone that he is a fool.

Then the fourth contrast—wisdom is better than running away:

> If the anger of the ruler rises against you, do not leave your place, for deference will make amends for great offenses (10:4).

There are times when running away looks like the best thing to do, but this text warns us that it isn't. It is much wiser to give a soft answer that turns away wrath, or to show deference— which means to acknowledge another person's feelings instead of your own—to whoever may be offended. Even a ruler or a king can be placated by deference.

Then in verses 5 through 7 we have the opposite of this, the hurt that foolish thinking can cause:

> There is an evil which I have seen under the sun, as it were an error proceeding from the ruler; folly is set in many high places, and the rich sit in a low place. I have seen slaves on horses, and princes walking on foot like slaves.

An error that those in authority often make is to appoint their incompetent friends to office; they put the wrong people in the right place. People who have no ability are exalted and put in high places, while those with great ability are treated like slaves and have no opportunity. Favoritism, this is called.

In one issue of *Time* magazine there was an article on the way political appointments have diminished the authority and prestige of the Supreme Court of California. This is the very problem this verse talks about.

In the next section, verses 8 through 11, the Searcher describes the kinds of insights that wisdom will embrace. First, there is counsel on avoiding dangers, understanding that certain situations have inherent dangers:

> He who digs a pit will fall into it, and a serpent will bite him who breaks through a wall. He who quarries stones is hurt by them, and he who splits logs is endangered by them (10:8).

Very few of us will ever be heavily involved in digging pits, breaking down walls, quarrying stones, or splitting logs. But these verses go beyond physical situations; they also describe the things we do to each other. Did you ever dig a pit for someone—lay a trap to embarrass him, to make him look bad or injure him in some way—only to find that you yourself were trapped by the situation you had designed? Wisdom understands that when you dig a pit you too are in danger. You may fall into it yourself.

Wisdom also understands that when you try to break down some wall of obstruction that keeps you from getting at someone or something, you are in danger, for hidden in that wall may be a serpent that will strike you. Many a person has discovered that in heavy-handedly trying to break down someone's resistance, he has triggered a serpent within that flashes up in anger and leads to hurtful, destructive consequences. He has been bitten through his own folly.

"He who quarries stones"—he who tries to remove something of value, to dig out something for himself that will be of great use and profit—must realize that he can be hurt by that. He may get what he wants, but it will be the worst thing that could happen to him. Psalm 106 says of the Israelites in the wilderness, "He (God) gave them their request, but he sent leanness into their soul."

"He who splits logs is endangered by them." Here is the same principle. The idea is that care must be taken in all these attempts to do things, since they may endanger you as well.

There follow two verses on how wisdom enlists help in time. First:

> *If the iron is blunt and one does not whet the*
> *edge, he must put forth more strength, but wisdom*
> *helps one to succeed (10:10).*

If you do not think through what you are going to do, and sharpen the edge of your approaches by pondering carefully how you are going to go about something, you will only expend a lot of effort and find yourself worn out in the process. But the wise man, understanding the need for sharpness and clarity, will whet the edge of his thought before he tries something, and will thus succeed.

Second:

> *If the serpent bites before it is charmed, there is*
> *no advantage in a charmer (10:11).*

The damage is already done. Do not go seeking counsel or help to remedy a situation after it has happened. Go for help before it is needed. Seek the counsel of one who can defuse the situation, one who can calm the serpent which is within all of us, before you get into trouble. That is the point of wisdom. How practical this is!

The passage closes with verses 12 through 15, where the Searcher sets forth the dangers of foolish talking:

> *The words of a wise man's mouth win him favor,*
> *but the lips of a fool consume him (10:12).*

When, without thinking, we follow the secular wisdom around us (wisdom that looks good and feels

right but nevertheless is foolish), we will end up hurting ourselves by what we say. How tragically this has
been illustrated in the lives of those who fling over-
board the wisdom of the Word and speak according
to the mind of the world. They end up broken and
hurting, wretched and miserable, defiled and de-
bauched or empty and lonely. The increasing misery
and anguish of life that we see around us is due to a
deliberate turning away from the wisdom of the mind
of God. That sort of mindset consumes, it destroys.

Furthermore, it escalates:

> *The beginning of the words of his mouth is
> foolishness, and the end of his talk is wicked mad-
> ness (10:13).*

Read the papers tomorrow morning and you will
see several illustrations of people who started out trying to express themselves in a simple way, but the
situation escalated until they resorted to violence,
even murder. This is the power of foolish speaking.
Such talk is often effusive:

> *A fool multiplies words, though no man knows
> what is to be, and who can tell him what will be
> after him? (10:14)*

One of the marks of foolish counsel is the prolixity
of it, of saying things for the sake of being heard. I
am reminded of the man who said, "All my wife ever
does is talk, talk, talk!" His friend asked, "What does
she talk about?" He replied, "I don't know; she won't
say!"

Words devoid of content—this is characteristic of
our time. There never was such a day in which people
were bombarded with so many words, so much litera-
ture, so much spouting of words through the media.
Yet much of it is thoroughly empty, unsatisfying and
misleading in the extreme.

So the Searcher closes the section,

> *The toil of a fool wearies him so that he does not*
> *know the way to the city (10:15).*

The fool doesn't know how to proceed; he is confused, weary, empty. So much of what we hear today leaves us like that. You run after these things and find they do not fulfill you. You do not feel strengthened. You spend hours looking at television, reading magazines, novels, or newspapers, yet you are not fed, you are not satisfied, strengthened, or helped. You feel empty, lonely, and depressed.

Worse than that, you are confused. Many are saying, "I don't know what to do about this problem; I don't know what steps to take." But the Scriptures tell you that in every situation where you need guidance there is a step to take, something you can do that is right. If you do the right, another step will open, then another, and soon you will find there is a Divine Hand guiding you step by step through the situation. Instead of breaking up, ruining and damaging your life, gradually the situation unfolds and leads to a solution. There comes a sense of joy and satisfaction that God has worked out the problem.

I have deliberately set this passage in the context of marriage, even though it applies to many other situations. I want you who are struggling with your marriages to know that God understands, he sympathizes, he knows it is difficult. But you are making a sad and sorry mistake if you resort to divorce. That is the world's way out, which ends in hurt and further confusion.

# 10
# HOW, THEN, SHOULD WE LIVE?

The title I have given to this study in Ecclesiastes 10 is the question, "How, Then, Should We Live?" Some may immediately recognize that this is a slight alteration of the title of a book by Dr. Francis Schaeffer. His way of putting the question is, "How Should We Then Live?" I have always been uncomfortable with the place which the word "then" occupies in that title. It makes me feel as I have felt when I have been a guest in someone's home and noticed a picture askew on the wall. As soon as my host left the room I jumped up, straightened the picture, and heaved a sigh of relief. So please forgive my impertinence in correcting the question to, "How, Then, Should We Live?"

That is a good question to ask at this point in our study of Ecclesiastes. In view of the new insights into life we have gained from this book, in view of the provision that God himself has made to supply to us directly the gift of enjoyment, we must ask, "How, Then, Should We Live?" That is the question the Searcher takes up as he draws near the close of his book.

The answer is threefold. He tells us, first, that we ought to live supportively; that is, to be responsible to work with others, especially with regard to government. Second, he tells us to live generously, to be warmly responsive to the needs of those around us. And third, we should live thoughtfully, responding daily to the truth that is taught in this book and throughout Scripture.

Live supportively! Live generously! Live thoughtfully!

Let us take the first one—*live supportively*—beginning with verse 16. This has to do with government. It is only natural that King Solomon would be much concerned about government. He was the Head of State in his day. We have noted that the Word of God gives many directions about the relationship between believers and the government. Clearly, government is part of God's plan for life.

King Solomon admits in this section that all government is not good:

> *Woe to you, O land, when your king is a child, and your princes feast in the morning! Happy are you, O land, when your king is the son of free men, and your princes feast at the proper time, for strength, and not for drunkenness! (10:16-17)*

Some governments ("administrations" is the word we would use) are hard to live with. They are headed by persons who are either incompetent, impulsive, and simpleminded, or naive, vain and insecure, or even untrustworthy and weak. The Watergate scandal is more than a decade old now, and we can see that much of the turmoil and trouble that we went through in those days stemmed from the insecurity and the untrustworthy character of the man who was president at the time. When Leon Jaworski, the Watergate Special Prosecutor, died, the news media reported on his career. I was struck by one thing that he said.

As he investigated the intrigue surrounding Watergate, the thing that struck him most forcefully was to hear President Nixon's instructions on a tape to one of his underlings on how to lie so as not to perjure himself. That struck Jaworski as a most serious revelation of the weakness of our former head of state.

That is what these words of Scripture represent as well. Some governments are weak; they do not have the kind of leadership we need.

Along with such inadequate leadership we often find a hierarchy of officials given over to self-indulgence and self-serving. Solomon speaks of that here when he writes, "your princes feast in the morning." In Hebrew culture the morning was to be used to judge the needs and problems of the people. Late afternoon and evening was the time for feasting. But here were men who indulged themselves all through the day, neglecting their duties to do so. Some administrations are like that, even in a democratic nation such as ours.

But we can also get good government. The Searcher tells us, "Happy are you, O land, when your king is the son of free men." The phrase, "son of free men," perhaps ought to be translated, "Your king is a free man." That is, he is free to be what he ought to be. He has control of himself; he is not a slave to his needs or his impulses. His subordinates will also reflect that. They are responsible people who take care of their duties and feast at the proper time—and then only to gain strength, not merely to get drunk.

The point of all this comes in the next two verses, which tell those who are seeking to be wise with God's wisdom how to react to government, whether it is good or bad. What should we do? Here are a couple of proverbs to guide us:

> *Through sloth the roof sinks in, and through indolence the house leaks (10:18).*

Does your house leak? If it does, you now know the reason for it! I had a leak in my roof for five years before it was finally fixed, so I must acknowledge that the verse is true. Here the Searcher compares the nation to a house. The application is that a people who are given over to industriousness, hard work and profitable-though-demanding labor are laying the foundation for stability in government, no matter what the leader is like. Without that foundation of hard work and readiness to work, the roof falls in— the house leaks. Then a nation is insecure, and subject to invasion.

The second proverb continues the same thought:

> *Bread is made for laughter, and wine gladdens life, and money answers everything (10:19).*

That sounds very up-to-date. But he is saying, of course, that even the legitimate, normal, proper joys of life—bread, which enables us to feast together, and wine, which gladdens life—is all made available by money: "Money answers everything." The idea is that money supplies everything that is needed, and money comes from hard and profitable work.

The way to enjoy the normal pleasures of life (and the way a nation keeps strong and healthy) is to be given over to a willingness to work, in order to have money rather than to be dependent on handouts. Running all through Scripture is a recognition of the value of labor. This touches on the question of a welfare state, and on the increasingly luxurious living standards of our day. It declares that what makes a nation healthy, despite even the weakness of its leaders, is industrious, hardworking citizens who are willing to pay their own way and put in full time at their jobs. That is the way to support the government.

He closes this section with a warning about complaining against government:

> *Even in your thought, do not curse the king, nor in your bedchamber curse the rich; for a bird of the air will carry your voice, or some winged creature tell the matter (10:20).*

There, I am sure, is the origin of the popular saying, "A little bird told me." This may also be the first recorded instance of the bugging of a home by the government! It clearly reflects the modern proverb, "Even the walls have ears."

"Do not curse the government, even in your bedchamber or in your innermost thoughts." This does not imply that if you do complain, it might get back to the king and he will be angry with you and punish you. Rather, it suggests that your constant complaining about leadership creates a condition that spreads dissatisfaction with and distrust of government.

We may be seeing something of that today. The present generation, by and large, distrusts the powers and rights of government. This may be because young people now entering their majority have heard us who are older grumbling so much about the government that they have learned to distrust it, to feel that it is an unnecessary evil, and to react violently against it.

I saw an article recently which predicted that soon no American president will be able to serve more than one term in office. The reason? The media so scrutinizes the president and criticizes so vehemently everything he does and every word he speaks that no president will be able to stand the glare of such adverse publicity. It will be impossible to elect him to office a second term because nobody will trust him.

This is a commentary in our time against too much examination of peoples' lives, especially too much criticism of what they do. The American way is to elect a man to office, give him six months to change everything, and if he does not do it, spend the next three and a half years complaining about it.

There is a destructive element in complaining and griping about what government does. What a difference it makes in the quality of government if we show our support for those who are in office! The appeal of the Searcher is that if you want to be wise—remembering all that God provides in life as revealed in this book—then live supportively of the government.

His second word of admonition is found in chapter 11, verses 1-6. Here the word is *live generously*:

> *Cast your bread upon the waters, for you will find it after many days. Give a portion to seven, or even to eight, for you know not what evil may happen on earth (11:1-2).*

The idea here is openhanded generosity. Give freely, wisely, but generously to the needs of those about. This phrase, "Cast your bread upon the waters," was a proverb in Israel for what looked like wasteful expenditure. No one would take good bread and throw it in the river; he would be regarded as a spendthrift for that. But here we are encouraged to do that very thing. This is not advising us to thoughtlessly and carelessly give away our money, spending it like a drunken sailor. What is meant is, "be willing to take a chance where a real need is evident."

When you see people in need, though you do not know how they may use your money—it may not be apparent that they will even use it wisely—nevertheless, be generous. That is what he is saying. "Cast your bread on the waters," take a chance, for in the wisdom and purpose of God it may very well return to you some day when you need help. I could relate several stories of people who have helped strangers, although they had no idea that their help was going to be used properly; then later when they found themselves in serious trouble, that person or that deed reappeared to help them. This is what the Searcher is encouraging.

Also, give as widely as possible: "Give a portion to seven, or even to eight, for you know not what evil may happen on earth." That is not limiting the number we should have on our help list. This Hebrew idiom, "Give a portion to seven or even to eight" is a way of saying, "Give to as many as you can, and then some." Be generous. Do not stop with a few close needs around you. Do not say, "I gave at the office," when someone asks for help at your door. You do not know what evil may be averted by your gift; that is the implication of this verse.

Giving is a way of relieving need, but oftentimes the need is not fully expressed. Sometimes we must be sensitive to where people are, and to the fact that in their pride they hide dire needs. But if we are generous in our giving, we often meet needs that we do not know anything about. If we spread it as wisely as we can, we continue to meet unknown needs in that way.

There follows four reasons for this kind of generosity. The Searcher again quotes some proverbs. Here are two good reasons, in verse 3:

> *If the clouds are full of rain, they empty themselves on the earth (nobody can contradict that in California!); and if a tree falls to the south or to the north, in the place where the tree falls, there it will lie.*

What does this mean? We must take this in the light of the context. The first reason that we are to give generously is because it is the natural outflow of a full life, like clouds filled with rain which empty themselves again and again upon the earth.

One winter I was entranced to watch the weather reports about Hurricane Iwa, which hit the Hawaiian Islands and dumped billions of gallons of water there. Then it moved across the Pacific and hit the West Coast, dumping more billions of gallons of water upon us. It moved up into the Sierras, then into the Rockies and across into the Plain States. It caused much flooding in Missouri, Arkansas and the Mississippi Valley. Then it moved on across the nation and dumped water again on the East Coast, passing out at last into the Atlantic.

Like clouds that are full of rain, a life that is full of the blessing and grace of God ought to shower many others with that blessing. Remember the words of Jesus, "Freely you have received, freely give." God has blessed us abundantly in this country. Despite an occasional recession we are still the richest nation on earth. The poorest among us are better off than the rich in many countries of the world. God has richly

blessed us. We are to give because it is the natural outflow of a life that is already filled with the blessings of
God, not only physically, but spiritually and emotionally as well.

The second parable, about the tree falling to the
south or north, is somewhat more difficult to inter-
pret. But one day I saw a motto in someone's kitchen
that captures exactly what this idiom teaches. It said,
"Bloom where you are planted." That is, it is God
who controls the fall of a tree in the forest; whether it
falls to the south or the north is determined by divine
providence. But where it falls, that is where it is to
be.

This is Solomon's way of saying to us, "Where God
has put you, right in your present circumstances, that
is where you are to give. Meet the needs around you.
Supply the needs of those with whom you come in
contact." That does not always mean geographically.
You may be in touch with someone halfway around
the world whose needs you are aware of, but God has
brought that to your knowledge so that you can meet
that need.

There is a third reason given in verse 4:

> _He who observes the wind will not sow; and he_
> _who regards the clouds will not reap._

That is, do not wait for the perfect time to give.
Do not wait until you have a certain figure in the bank
before you start giving. This is a good word for young
people. You sometimes think that because you have a
limited income you cannot give; but if you wait until
you get enough to live on, you will never give. Give
as the need arises, as the opportunity comes, as far as
you can. That is the exhortation here.

Finally, a fourth reason, a very insightful one, appears in verses 5 and 6:

*As you do not know how the spirit comes to the bones in the womb of a woman with child, so you do not know the work of God who makes everything. In the morning sow your seed, and at evening withhold not your hand; for you do not know which will prosper, this or that, or whether both alike will be good.*

Twice in those verses is the phrase, "you do not know." We have seen many times in this book the mystery connected with life. There is much we do not know. One of the things no one has yet understood, even in this scientific age, is "how the spirit comes to the bones in the womb of a woman with child." How does the human personality, that which distinguishes us from the beasts, form in the yet unborn fetus? No one knows, but it is present; the child is a human being.

This is another verse that clearly supports the anti-abortion movement of today, for it indicates beyond doubt that a fetus is a person.

These verses point up our lack of understanding of the power of God. We do not know how he uses gifts, but he does—and he uses them in remarkable ways. Remember the story of Jesus observing the people throwing their money into the temple treasury? One woman threw in two pennies, two mites, the smallest coin in Israel. Yet of her Jesus said, "This woman has cast in more than all the others who have given." Many have puzzled over those words. Two mites are hardly a drop in the bucket compared with the wealth that may have been put into that treasury that day.

What did Jesus mean? What he said was literally true. That story from the lips of Jesus has been repeated all over the earth, in every culture and clime. For two thousand years it has been told again and again. It has motivated more people to give than any other story ever told. Thus it is true that in the wisdom and power of God that tiny gift was so multiplied that it has outweighed all the giving of any single gift from any individual, no matter how rich, throughout the history of Christendom.

That is the power of God to use our gifts. We do not know what he is going to do with the money and the help that we give.

Nor do we understand the timing of God. You cannot say that a gift given at some prosperous time in your life—larger than you could give at any other time—is going to be used more of God than any small gift you present. You cannot tell whether the fifty cents or dollar given when you were in high school or college may be used of God to produce great benefit in the lives of others, or that something given in old age might not do the same thing. We do not know the power of God or the timing of God. But we are encouraged to give, because "God loves a cheerful giver." He changes and blesses lives, he changes the history of the world by the phenomenon of Christian giving. So *live generously* says the Searcher.

A third exhortation says *live thoughtfully.*

> *Light is sweet, and it is pleasant for the eyes to behold the sun. For if a man lives many years, let him rejoice in them all; but let him remember that the days of darkness will be many. All that comes is vanity (11:7-8).*

Light and sun are symbols of life lived in the love of God. Just as we like to step outside when we see the sun break through on a cloudy, gloomy day, so we can remind ourselves of the love of God, the sense of his acceptance, the joy of his presence, the feeling that we are approved and accepted by him. "Keep yourselves in the love of God," says Jude, the Lord's brother. This is what makes life beautiful, enjoyable, and gives cause for rejoicing all our days. It is what makes life worth living.

We have seen all through this book that enjoyment does not come from things. "The days of darkness will be many," Solomon tells us. It is difficult to see whether this refers to the times of trial and problems in life, or whether it may refer (as I think it may) to the ending of our earthly life. That is what it goes on to speak of in the next chapter. Life is given to us for enjoyment, but the secret of it, as we have seen many times already, is not possessions. Jesus underscored that: "A man's life does not consist of the abundance of things which he possesses." It is rather a relationship with a Living God. Let us rejoice because of that.

In the final two verses of the chapter, Solomon spells out some advice for young people:

> *Rejoice, O young man, in your youth, (the Hebrew expression includes women as well) and let your heart cheer you in the days of your youth; walk in the ways of your heart and the sight of your eyes. But know that for all these things God will bring you into judgment. Remove vexation from your mind, and put away pains from your body (literally, instead of "pains from your body," it is "evil from your flesh"); for youth and the dawn of life are vanity (11:9-10).*

This sounds as if God is offering life with one hand and taking it back with the other: "But know that God will bring you into judgment." It is really an encouragement to realize that it is God that has given the gift of youth, with its strength, its optimism, its cheer, its dreams, its hopes, its opportunities.

I am continually amazed at the energy of young

people. We have three little grandsons living with us. When I come home, weary and tired, although they have been tearing around all day they still want to wrestle me on the floor of the living room. Sometimes I heave a sigh of relief when they finally give up and go to bed. Some of us who are older like to quote George Bernard Shaw, "Youth is such a wonderful thing it is a shame to waste it on young people."

The point of this is that God gives the gift of youth, so rejoice in it, enjoy it, use it. Relish the strength of it, the cheerfulness of it, the optimism of it. Young people, for the most part, believe that everything is going to turn out all right, so they energetically pursue things. This verse encourages that.

Youth is properly the time to plan, to try new things, to explore new opportunities, new adventures. In my twenties I had the opportunity, following the outbreak of World War II, to go to the Hawaiian Islands and work in industry there. It seemed to me a great and enticing opportunity to see new places. I have always been grateful that I did that in my twenties, when I could enjoy it to the full. I believe that this is what this verse is telling us to do. Youth is the time to seize opportunities and to follow our desires.

But . . . (there is always a but, isn't there?) remember that ultimately there must be an accounting. This is a parallel to Paul's word in 2 Corinthians, "We must all (all believers) appear before the judgment seat of Christ, that we may receive the things done in the body, whether they be good or bad." This book will close with that reminder again.

> *For God will bring every deed into judgment, with every secret thing, whether good or evil (12:14).*

That is not a threat. It is simply a guide, a reminder to youth that though there are great, open doors of opportunity flung wide open now, they will not always be there. Therefore enter them with the realization that you must make wise choices. You must deny yourself the pleasures of sin; you must make choices in the light of how your life will ultimately be evaluated.

In verse 10, the Searcher specifies exactly what he means. Here is what a young person ought to do. First, "Remove vexation from your mind." Vexation is a word that combines the thoughts of anger and resentment. This is one of the great problems of youth. Young people tend to be angry and resentful when things don't go the way they'd like. God is warning them not to be trapped by that. That is what makes young people rebel; that is what often makes them plunge into distressful and dangerous situations and hurtful experiences. So "remove vexation from your mind." Do not let it gnaw away at your spirit and thus find yourself an angry young man or a resentful young woman, not liking what God has given you or where he has put you.

Second, "put away evil from your flesh." Stop bad and harmful practices. Put away dangerous things—drugs, wrongful use of your sexual powers, damaging things, smoking, drinking, whatever they are—stop them! That is what he says. That is to live thoughtfully in the midst of life.

Remember, too, that "youth and the dawn of life are vanity." Even that glorious experience of youth is not the reason why life was given. This, again, challenges the secular illusions that we are subjected to all the time. The media blares that youth is the great idol, the thing to seek for. Youth is held up for us to emulate. We are exposed to a thousand ways to find the secret of recovering or preserving our youth: "Buy this new salve or perfume; take this course or use this device, and your youth will be preserved." But youth, according to the wise words of Scripture, is in itself empty. It is not vitality that satisfies, but a relationship with God. So the Searcher goes on to say in the closing chapter, "Remember your Creator in the days of your youth."

How, then, should we live? Live supportively with regard to the government; live generously with regard to the hurts and needs of those around you; and live thoughtfully as you daily make the choices and decisions of life.

# 11
# BEFORE IT'S
# TOO LATE

The Searcher of Israel was concerned that we who read his book might find our way out of the tragedies, the troubles, the difficulties and the dangers of life before it is too late. Before the flame of our life burns out he wants us to find the secret of living. So he continues in this last chapter with a further word to youth:

*Remember also your Creator in the days of your youth, before the evil days come, and the years draw nigh, when you will say, "I have no pleasure in them" ( 12:1 ).*

This is an appeal to young people to think often and seriously about their Creator, not simply to remember that he is there. The idea is: Recall God's presence daily, live in a relationship with him, seek to discover the greatness and glory of God while you are still young . . . before it is too late.

Before we develop that thought, let us first read the verses that follow, for these give the reason for thinking about and relating to God while one is still young. That reason is, "evil days are coming."

Those evil days are described in verses 2 through 8 by a vivid and beautiful imagery which describes the aging process, and the decrepitude of old age. Remember your Creator . . .

> *. . . before the sun and the light and the moon and the stars are darkened and the clouds return after the rain; in the day when the keepers of the house tremble, and the strong men are bent, and the grinders cease because they are few, and those that look through the windows are dimmed, and the doors on the street are shut; when the sound of the grinding is low, and one rises up at the voice of a bird, and all the daughters of song are brought low; they are afraid also of what is high, and terrors are in the way; the almond tree blossoms, the grasshopper drags itself along and desire fails; before man goes to his eternal home, and the mourners go about the streets; before the silver cord is snapped, or the golden bowl is broken, or the pitcher is broken at the fountain, or the wheel broken at the cistern, and the dust returns to the earth as it was, and the spirit returns to God who gave it. Vanity of vanities, says the Preacher; all is vanity.*

In marvelous poetry the Searcher describes the increasing weaknesses of old age and the actual experi-

ence of death. Since this is where life is headed for all
of us, he admonishes, "remember your Creator in the
days of your youth."

Let us go through these verses again and see exactly
what he describes. Most commentators agree that the
words, "before the sun and the light and the moon
and the stars are darkened and the clouds return after
the rain," refer to the fading of mental powers as one
grows older.

When you are young, life seems to stretch endlessly before you. It seems that you will never grow
old. But as you live through the years, life seems to
speed by more rapidly, and at last it feels like it is very
brief. Suddenly you find yourself looking and feeling
old. As someone has said, "About the time your face
clears up, your mind begins to go!" That is how brief
life appears to be.

The mental faculties are described here in terms of
light. The mind, with its powers of reasoning, of
memory and of imagination, begins to fade like the
dying rays of a setting sun. The reasoning power of
the brain, perhaps the greatest gift that God has
given to us, begins to lose its skill. Memory fades—
that is one of the first marks of old age. This verse
describes the failing of memory and of the imagination, like the stars which fade at the approaching
dawn.

"The clouds returning after the rain," is a reference
to the second childhood, the senility which comes on
in old age. As a child, life revolves around three
simple things: eating, sleeping, and going to the
bathroom. In the aged that same cycle returns.

Then the Searcher speaks of "the day when the
keepers of the house tremble." The keepers of the
house are the arms and the hands by which we defend
ourselves if attacked. They are useful in maintaining

the body, which begins to bend and tremble in old age. Old people take very short steps; they sometimes can hardly walk. One sign of the onset of old age is when your knees buckle but your belt won't. Some of us are beginning to exhibit those signs.

Then he speaks of "the grinders ceasing because they are few." That needs no interpretation for those who have already lost many of their grinders through tooth decay. Mealtimes are prolonged because it takes so long to get food lined up with the few remaining grinders!

"Those that look through the windows are dimmed" clearly refers to the fading of eyesight as old age approaches. Cataracts form. Various eye problems develop. Almost all lose the ability to read close up; we must hold things at arm's length to see what they are.

"The doors on the street are shut" is a vivid picture of what happens when the teeth fall out. The doors of the face, the lips, fall in. When that happens "the doors to the street" obviously shut.

"When the sound of the grinding is low" is thought by some commentators to refer to the digestive system. But because we have already identified the "grinders" as the teeth, it seems better to say that this is a reference to how the aged, now toothless, gum their food. That does not result in a lot of noise! It is hard to chew Grape Nuts when you have no teeth!

Then, "one rises up at the voice of a bird." I have noticed that in the mornings any sound will waken me. It is characteristic of the aged, who are easily awakened. Even the sound of chirping of birds outside the window awakens them.

Yet, at the same time, "all the daughters of song are brought low." That refers to the increasing deafness of old age. "The daughters of song" are the ears, through which we hear song. They are brought low; they lose their powers. Everybody seems to talk in a much lower tone than they used to. People seem to mumble as "the daughters of song are brought low."

Next is a word on the increasing fears of old age: "They are afraid also of what is high, and terrors are in the way." Older people fear almost every step. They are afraid of the cracks in the sidewalk. They are afraid to mount stairs. They are afraid of "what is high." Terrors increase as they go about the streets. Older people tend to stay in. They do not even want to drive at night because they are afraid of "terrors in the way."

"The almond tree blossoms" is a clear reference to the hair, which turns white with old age. Like the white blossoms of the almond tree, one begins to take on a very different look as age advances.

I never understood until recently what was meant by "the grasshopper drags itself along." But when I wake in the morning now I find myself stiff, and sometimes I have difficulty walking. This increases as one grows old. It results in the infirm and feeble steps of the very aged. "The grasshopper drags itself along."

Finally, "desire fails." That is a reference to sexual desire. It may be a great comfort to many of you to see that this is last on the list! It is the last thing to go, according to this statement.

Let us acknowledge that modern technology has helped solve many of these problems. We can buy wigs when our hair falls out, or dentures when our teeth rot away. Glasses, contact lenses, and even glass eyes help with vision problems. Artificial legs, arms, and hands can be fitted. All of these are great devices. With all the help that modern technology avails, it

must be quite a sight when some people get ready for
bed. It would be like watching the demolition of a
house!

Still, we have not moved very far from the days of
the Searcher, even though we have devised many ways
to disguise aging. Even with these modern helps,
Solomon's words are a revelation of the up-to-
dateness of Scripture.

The Searcher goes on to describe the various ways
death can occur. In frankness and openness the Scripture faces the fact that "Man goes to his eternal
home." Despite the many passages in this book in
which the writer seems to see death as the end of all
the good things under the sun, that is, in this life,
nevertheless there are several statements that human
existence goes on beyond death. Here is one of them:
"Man goes to his eternal home." The grave is not the
end! There is life, there is existence, beyond death.

Meanwhile, "the mourners go about the streets."
This, the Searcher says, is a result of the various forms
death takes. First, "the silver cord is snapped." That
seems clearly a reference to the spinal cord, that great
nerve that runs up and down our backs, protected by
our spines. If it is damaged, broken, or diseased, life
can suddenly end.

Or "the golden bowl is broken." That is a reference
to the cranium, the skull. A blow to the head damaging the brain may destroy an essential part of our
earthly existence, suddenly ending life.

"The pitcher is broken at the fountain" is a reference to the heart. Heart disease, cardiac arrest, is the
most frequent cause of death in the United States
today. The heart can suddenly stop—the fountain
which continually pours blood through our bodies
can break and cease to function.

"The wheel broken at the cistern" refers to the circulation of the blood. The continual wheel of life which keeps us alive can stop through degeneration of the veins, through hardening of the arteries, or through a blood clot. Sudden death can occur.

The result of any of these failures is that the body crumbles: "Dust returns to the earth as it was." But "the spirit" —the part of our humanity which differentiates us from the animals, that part which seeks after eternity, for something beyond life, that part which is restless and empty within us when we have not found the key to life—"the spirit returns to God who gave it." What an accurate and vivid description this is of the ending of life!

The Searcher's conclusion, then, is the same one we have seen throughout the book. Life "under the sun," lived without having discovered the reason for living, is vanity, emptiness, futility. The greatest futility is a life that has not found a reason for living. What a waste, to live and never discover why you are here! What a waste, to die without learning the secret of true existence! That is the Searcher's ultimate conclusion. He began the book with it, in verse 2, and ends here in verse 8 of chapter 12 with the same words. He has searched through all of life and has reached his conclusion.

To return to verse 1 of this chapter, it is hard to find the answer to life when you're old, and not many do. There are stories (thank God for every one of them) of people turning to God in their last moments. Some of us know someone who did that in a real and genuine way. But it does not happen frequently. Statistics show that most people who come to Christ come while they are relatively young. Ninety-five percent of all believers come to Christ before they are 50 years old, and most of those before they are 30.

Youth is the time to find God. That is what Solomon tells us: "Remember your Creator in the days of your youth."

Remembering God means to relate to him, to walk with him, to discover him, to learn to know him while you are young. There are two excellent reasons given for this.

First, because "evil days are coming." Old age is setting in, and you will lose your ability to change and learn new things. There probably has never been a time when youth has been subjected to more temptations and pressures to wrong living than today. Temptation is all around us, subtle and powerful. The appeal of the world and the flesh is constantly with us, turning thousands of young people away from the truth of God. But bad as it is when you are young, it will get worse the older you grow. The pressures to conform are greater when you move out into life and business, when you become parents, when you become breadwinners and establish homes. The pressures to conform, to fit in with the ways of the world, will be far more intense then than they are while you are in high school or college. Evil pressures increase—that is one good reason to remember your Creator in the days of your youth.

Second, your motivations are highest now. The Searcher says days are coming "when you will say, 'I'm not motivated at all.'" One of the signs of age is its unwillingness to change, its resistance to new ideas. I have often observed the tragedy of older people who acknowledge they've missed the secret of life, but who are unwilling to change simply because it is so hard to do when they are old. This is why the Searcher exhorts young people, "Learn about God now; open your heart to him; seek the wisdom of God now. Study the Scriptures now, when you are young, while motivation is high and evil pressures are less, and you can discover the secret of living while you are still young enough to enjoy the blessing it will bring."

We have a wonderful example of this in Jesus. He grew up in a godly home, was exposed to the truth of the Scripture, involved himself with the work of his father in the carpenter's shop. The one thing that is recorded of him in those days is that "He grew in favor with God and man."

Jesus put God first in his life. He understood the key to life, the secret of learning how to handle the problems and pressures of life. And what is that? It is to be in relationship and touch with the Living God who is at work in the affairs of men. Jesus saturated his mind with the Scriptures. He could quote them from memory at any time in his ministry because his mind was filled with what God had said. And he understood these marvelous words.

When he was only twelve years old he astonished the doctors in the temple by his wisdom, asking them penetrating questions they could never answer. He went back with his mother and father to finish his boyhood in Nazareth, having "remembered his Creator in the days of his youth."

The last five verses of this book are an epilogue. The Searcher takes us back over the entire book and reminds us of the careful search he made to come to his conclusion.

> Besides being wise, the Preacher also taught the people knowledge, weighing and studying and arranging proverbs with great care. The Preacher sought to find pleasing words and uprightly he wrote words of truth (12:9-10).

This revealing verse reminds us how carefully this book has been compiled. Solomon himself learned to be wise. The only source of that wisdom, he tells us, was the Word of God. He sought through the Scriptures, learned them, and then taught the people.

This knowledge of the Scriptures enabled the Searcher to teach with great power and influence—but only after careful preparation. Notice what he did: "He arranged these proverbs with great care." Throughout the book are many proverbs which he uses to illustrate the truth he sets forth. They were not lightly chosen. They were not haphazardly arranged. We must take them seriously. They are not mere one-liners, meant to amuse. They are carefully chosen and arranged to illustrate what he had to say.

More than that, he sought for arresting, accurate words to express this wisdom. This is a great verse for teachers and preachers. It will help them understand what is necessary for public ministry. Not only must we have an understanding of the subject, but we must think through how to say it in such a way that people will listen. That is how the Searcher proceeded. It is excellent advice.

He underscores the value of Scripture in picturesque terms.

> *The sayings of the wise are like goads, and like nails firmly fixed are the collected sayings which are given by one Shepherd. My son, beware of anything beyond these. Of making many books there is no end, and much study is a weariness of the flesh (12:11-12).*

All students will say "Amen!" to that word: "Much study is a weariness of the flesh." But notice how he describes the value of Scripture. It is like a "goad." It prods and pokes you, you cannot get it out of your mind. It makes you go where you would not ordinarily go. It works by prodding you along.

I suspect many have discovered that aspect of Scripture. I once knew a man who was in the grip of a terrible depression for more than a year. It had destroyed his marriage. He had lost his job and could not function. But he was delivered by daily meditating on a simple statement he found in Scripture, the only Scripture he could believe at the time, the words of Jesus, "Not my will but thine be done." Thinking on that day after day prodded him, goaded him to think about his own life. He came out of his depression within a relatively short time and never returned to it again. That is how Scripture works.

It is also a "nail( an anchor) firmly fixed." You can hang on to it and hold fast to it in times of danger and temptation. Once when I was severely troubled and so deeply disturbed that I could not even eat, one phrase from the lips of Jesus came to my mind again and again. It was the phrase in the fourteenth chapter of John, when Jesus said to his worried disciples, "Let not your heart be troubled."

I was gripped by those two words, "Let not." They said to me that a troubled heart is subject to the will of that believer. He can let his heart be troubled or he can let it not be troubled. The ground for letting it not be troubled is in the words that immediately follow: "You believe in God, believe also in me." When the realization struck me that my Lord was there with me with wisdom and power to handle the situation, I felt my heart's load lifted. I was free to let not my heart be troubled. That is the power of Scripture.

Why does it have this unique power? Why does it, more than any other book, have this ability? The reason, according to verse 11, is that "the collected sayings are given by one Shepherd." These are

inspired, God-breathed words. The heart of God is
the heart of a shepherd; he sees us as wandering sheep
in need of a shepherd's care. The shepherd-character
of our Lord is probably the reason why the shepherds
of Bethlehem were chosen to be the first men to hear
the wonderful words of the angels, "This day is born
to you in the city of David a Savior, who is Christ the
Lord."

The shepherds would understand, as Isaiah says,
"All we like sheep have gone astray. We have turned
every one to his own way." But the hope that was
awakened on that Christmas morning was the realization that the One who was born in the manger was
the One of whom it was said, "the Lord shall lay upon
him the iniquities of us all." That is where hope
comes in life.

"Do not go beyond that, " the Searcher warns. This
is the word of wisdom to scholars and all searchers for
knowledge: "Of making many books there is no end."
You can read yourself to death. You can study yourself
to death. Scripture is not saying that study is wrong.
No, it is right to read and search and know and learn.
But beware of letting this take you beyond what this
book so clearly declares, that God is the secret of life,
that he is the reason for existence. Until we discover
him, study and books will never be of any continuing
value to us.

This is clearly and finally stated in the two closing
verses of the book:

> *The end of the matter: all has been heard. Fear
> God, and keep his commandments; for this is the
> whole duty of man (12:13).*

Remove the word "duty" from your version. It is
not in the Hebrew, even though every version seems

to use that unfortunate translation. It is really this statement:

> *Fear God, and keep his commandments; for this*
> *is the wholeness of man.*

The secret of wholeness is to "Fear God, and keep his commandments." It is to discover the secret of being a whole person. Who does not want that? We desire to be whole, not broken, fragmented, easily upset, erratic, going off in all directions at once. But we want to be stable, controlled, balanced, whole people. Here is the secret of it. This is what we are to learn when we are young: "Remember your Creator in the days of your youth," before the pressures come upon you. It is the secret of wholeness: "Fear God, and keep his commandments."

Everything hangs upon the word, "Fear God." This is a difficult idea for us. Most of us think of fear as abject terror, as running from God because he is a threat. But that is never the biblical meaning of the word. Put in the form of an acrostic it becomes easier to remember:

**F** stands for *faith in his existence*. You cannot come to God unless you know he is there. Hebrews 11:6 declares, "He that comes to God must believe that he is and that he is a rewarder of those that diligently seek him." There is where fear begins— faith that God exists. The whole of the created universe shouts this at us. The inner responses of our heart confirm it. The Word of God declares it and history reveals it. Francis Schaeffer says that this is the great and first truth of the gospel—the God who is there!

**E** is the *experience of his grace*. You never can properly fear God until you have learned for yourself what kind of a God he is. He is a God of mercy, of grace, of forgiveness. When you have stood before him and felt your guilt, when you have known you were wrong and corrupt, and heard him say in your inner heart, "neither do I condemn you; go and sin no more," then you will be able to properly fear God. One element of fear is the experience of the wonder of forgiveness, that God forgives and sends you out again with a new purpose and a new resource.

That leads to the third element: **A** is *awe at the majesty, the wisdom and wonder of God*. What a Being he is! What a marvelous mind that comprehends the billions of pieces of information in this universe and holds them continually before him. What power to hear every voice and relate to every person who has ever lived! What a marvelous God! Awe before his majesty, before his comprehensiveness, before his un-failing wisdom and power. That is part of fearing God.

The last letter, **R** stands for *resolve to do what he says, to obey his word, to keep his commandments*. Jesus himself said that. All the law and the writings can be reduced to two simple things, he said: "Love the Lord your God with all your heart and all your soul and all your mind." That is to be done in response to his love already shown to you. Love him because he first loved you. And second, "Love mercy and walk humbly before your God." That is to obey him, to follow him, to keep his commandments. That is what it means to fear God.

> *Faith*
> *Experience*
> *Awe*
> *Resolve*

The Searcher concludes that nothing can be hid from God's eyes:

> *God will bring every deed into judgment, with
> every secret thing, whether good or evil (12:14).*

No one can hide from God. He is there in all our life. He knows everything that goes on, he knows the thought of the heart, every word of the mouth. He knows the motives that we seek to hide from others. He sees the duplicity, the deception, the lovelessness. He has made a record of it all; nothing can be hid. Everything will come out in the open at last. The illusions by which we seek to convince ourselves that things are not the way the Bible says they are will be stripped away and we will see ourselves as he sees us. And there will not be a voice lifted to challenge the righteousness of his judgment.

Because of that, Solomon exhorts us to fear God, to have faith in his existence, to experience his grace, to stand in awe of his Person, and to resolve to obey him. That is the secret to life. That is the secret of wholeness in man.

And with that King Solomon's record of lifelong research is finished. He writes at the end of a life which has known both leaping, flashing moments of pleasure, and long, lonely hours of shame and misery.

The record is plain for all to see. Life without God is dull, empty, vain. Life with him is full and satisfying. Even the tears and pain have meaning and value when we see they are chosen by him. The purpose behind it all is the increase of joy.